Tangible Compassion

Take note that the name "satan" and related names are not capitalized. We choose not to acknowledge him, even to the point of violating accepted grammatical rules.

ISBN 13 TP: 978-1-6631-0298-0

foreword by
DR. KEVIN ZADAI

Tangible Compassion

Becoming a Conduit of God's Love to a Broken World

Teri Camp Willis,
PhD, ThD

Dedication

I dedicate this book to my 94-year-old mom, Pearl Ella Camp, in love, honor, and gratitude. You are truly an authentic woman of God. I watched and experienced the Lord's tangible compassion flowing through you and into the lives of your family and countless others. Thank you for modeling life in Christ and for raising me to love, serve, and worship the one true and living God. Thank you for teaching me that I can do all things with the help and strength of Christ Jesus.

This book is also dedicated to my daughter, Taylor Ashley. Thank you for making me a mom and for being a compassionate leader for Christ to your generation.

I also thank Drs. Kevin and Kathi Zadai and Warrior Notes School of Ministry for making this book possible. Thank you for teaching, stretching, and mentoring me at a pivotal time in my life. I am forever grateful for your generosity and labor of love.

In loving memory of
my compassionate dad,
Frank Arthur Camp, Jr.

❧

Table of Contents

Foreword

As President of Warrior Notes School of Ministry, I have the privilege of witnessing the extraordinary ways in which our students thrive through learning, growth, and a shared commitment to Jesus Christ that is rooted in love, compassion, and humility. It is with great joy that I introduce *Tangible Compassion,* a book that is both a guide and companion on the deeply personal journey of spiritual growth. This book, written by Teri Camp Willis, one of our own graduates, reflects the very essence of these truths and offers you a unique opportunity to deepen your relationship with God and experience His transformative power in your everyday life.

At its core, *Tangible Compassion* invites you to step into the fullness of God's love—a love that not only heals but empowers. Teri offers practical insights on how to align yourself with God's purpose through repentance, emotional healing, and the pursuit of peace and joy. With each chapter, we are called to release limiting beliefs, choose forgiveness, and embrace the reality of Heaven on earth, all the while walking in the footsteps of Christ's example of humility, service, and selflessness.

As you read through this book, you will notice a consistent theme: the importance of a humble, teachable heart. It is through humility that we are able to see the world—and those around us—with the eyes of compassion. Teri beautifully articulates how emotional safety through Christ, resilience, and spiritual discipline are essential for flourishing in faith. The profound truth that true spiritual maturity is not just a set of beliefs, but a lifestyle marked by mercy, forgiveness, and unconditional love is something that will resonate deeply with all who seek a life that reflects God's goodness.

Tangible Compassion offers practical steps to cultivate the mind of Christ, resist the weight of worry, and embrace a life of joy and peace. Through each page, you are encouraged to cultivate emotional healing as you strengthen your relationship with Jesus. The transformative power of worship and praise—especially the healing found in singing—is another key point of focus, reminding us that our worship can bridge the gap between our hearts and the heart of God, bringing healing in ways we may not even fully understand.

As you journey through this book, I encourage you to approach it with an open heart—ready to embrace the transformative power of God's love. Let this be more than just a reading experience. Let it be a catalyst for deep, lasting change in your life. I pray that you find peace, strength, and renewed joy as you discover the beauty of living with a teachable, humble heart before God.

Dr. Kevin Zadai

Warrior Notes

Introduction

We have all heard that God is love, and that is absolute truth. However, His love is not an abstract theory; rather, this love, this compassion, is *tangible.* God's compassion for us and through us to others can be tasted, touched, and experienced. His love is a healing river of life that is continuously flowing from His throne like Niagara Falls times infinity. This book is full of life strategies that will help you thrive in the center of the deluge of His love, engulfed in His glorious presence. Only then can you become equipped and proficient in ruling and reigning over the darkness while still flourishing in every season.

The seasons that bring trouble, tragedy, and trauma often leave behind the residue of very painful, lingering emotions. No matter where you may have become imprisoned by what you've gone through, hope lies within these pages to eliminate every barrier so you can fully recover. Understanding what it means to live in the Spirit from the most truthful perspective while honing resiliency skills will speed up your healing process. It's one thing to have heard about God's easy yoke and light burden. (See Matthew 11:30.) However, it's a completely different thing to experience His supernatural ease in the midst of a really tough and dark battle.

The first goal of this book is to highlight actionable ways you can enlarge your capacity to receive comfort, healing, strength, and transformation from God's amazing love, regardless of the season you're in currently. As a licensed clinical pastoral counselor with a master's in clinical Christian counseling, a doctorate in Integrated Psychology, and a doctorate in Bible and Theology, I am not one who values worthless theories and philosophies or a powerless religion. I treasure sound wisdom and truth that have been proven to help and strengthen me every day in spite of challenges. The strategies found in these pages have steadied, enriched, and transformed my own life as well as the lives of those whom I have been entrusted to counsel and mentor.

In one chapter, I share a personal testimony of how I tested every truth, mindset, resiliency skill, and life strategy that I teach in this book during a three-year crisis. Not only did these all work, but I also was strengthened and sharpened within the very season that was intended to take me out. At the end of the day, church attendance, memorized scriptures, and accredited degrees are all worthless unless we actually trust God at a heart level and our minds are synced with the mind of Christ. In other words, we all need practical ways of personalizing and implementing Heaven's liberating truth and power into our lives. Without embodying biblical truth and acquiring resiliency skills to help maintain stability, there will be no lasting peace or freedom. Therefore, to help integrate this truth into our lifestyle, each chapter ends with a practical life application section.

Understanding how to adequately tend to the three parts of ourselves (spirit, soul, and body) is the only way to maintain absolute steadiness as the storms of life blow.

Later, I share another personal testimony of how I nearly died as a child. This time was the beginning of the Lord's tuning my heart to hear His whispers, a skill that preserved my life. Yet, the Lord is *much* greater, more powerful, and more loving than the sum of my personal experiences. Everyone is invited into an authentic relationship with the Lord to receive unconditional love and unlimited blessings as we each fulfill our destiny.

I've never met anyone who did not enjoy at least one genre of music. That's probably because we were created to worship God. Secondly, we've all experienced music's healthy benefits. However, music can be life-giving or harmful, depending on many variables, including the lyrics and the frequency. For those who enjoy singing, this book will inspire you to turn your melodies into mighty weapons that win any war, while simultaneously filling your entire being with supernatural peace.

Lastly, my prayer is that the entire family of God will mature in Christ-like character by understanding that there is no such thing as a spiritually safe Christian who is not *also* emotionally safe. Jesus is emotionally safe, and I strongly believe that we in the body of Christ will need this truth to become essential in our hearts when we are meeting the most important basic human needs of people, which are to feel loved, valued, and safe. In other words, as people experience Christ in us, He is revealed as the most valuable gift from God. He draws everyone into salvation and wholeness by His love. (See John 12:32.)

Let us heal and move forward in our purpose. Let us become transformed by the truth, cultivate joy, and choose humility and love as our mode of operation. Then we can become conduits of God's tangible compassion and supernatural power. We can live unencumbered and available for His glorious compassion to be poured through us and into the lives of others.

Chapter 1

Conduits of Compassion

The Lord wrote a book about our individual destiny prior to breathing us into our mother's womb. Our lives were not some careless afterthought, regardless of the circumstances surrounding our conception. We were all sent to a dysfunctional earth and into the lives of flawed, imperfect parents. However, once we reach adulthood, it is our responsibility to trust God to fill in any gaps in our upbringing and to heal any trauma. We are under the mercy of a loving, merciful God who does not have any grandchildren. We are children of God who were created in His image. (See Genesis 1:27.) The body, which only houses our spirit, is the part that shares our parents' DNA.

Total submission to the Lord and His healing process allows us to live unencumbered and increases our capacity to love and serve others well. It is up to us to live connected to Him for our daily supply and guidance. He is never going to give anyone a full blueprint of the day, year, or decade ahead. He is looking for an all-day, everyday trust and reliance on Him. His only motivation is that we would have access to His perfect love, exceptional wisdom, and help every moment of our lives.

> *You made all the delicate, inner parts of my body and knit me together in my mother's womb. Thank you for making me so wonderfully complex! Your workmanship is marvelous—how well I know it. You watched me as I was being formed in utter seclusion, as I was woven together in the dark of the womb. You saw me before I was born. Every day of my life was recorded in your book. Every moment was laid out before a single day had passed.* (Psalm 139:13–16 NLT)

The Lord planned a great life for us with ultimate victory over the adversary and restoration after every challenging season. However, He never promised that life on earth, even as a Christian, would be free from trouble. He only promised to be with us, strengthening and helping us to overcome every trial. We have access to courage, peace, and hope, even in crisis, from the posture of trusting Him and resting in His faithfulness. At the same time, there will be no rest without trust and no trust without humility and faith. The Lord's perfect love, grace, wisdom, and truth are consistently available. The choice to trust and follow His supernatural help is completely up to us.

> *And everything I've taught you is so that the peace which is in me will be in you and will give you great confidence as you rest in me. For in this unbelieving world you will experience trouble and sorrows, but you must be courageous, for I have conquered the world!* (John 16:33 TPT)

His manifested compassion is always available to help us as individuals and to help us to love and serve others. Even Jesus Christ was sent to earth filled with purpose to be a servant of all. "For even the Son of Man came not to be served but to serve others and to give his life as a ransom for many" (Matthew 20:28 NLT).

There will be no rest without trust and no trust without humility and faith.

❧

Authentic Compassion

True compassion is an action with an undeniable tangibility. It is not just a sympathetic, warm fuzzy feeling inside of our hearts. For example, praying for someone is kind and "helpful," but it does little for a person who is in desperate need of food or clothing. In that case, the most loving, helpful response is to actually provide food and clothing or the resources to attain them. However, we simply can't give away what we haven't first received, whether that's peace, food, financial assistance, or love. Therefore, until we receive the Lord's transformative love—which is well able to save, heal, and liberate us—our capacity to help others will be limited. His ways of ruling and reigning in life are more brilliant and more powerful than our best effort.

> *My dear brothers and sisters, what good is it if someone claims to have faith but demonstrates no good works to prove it? How could this kind of faith save anyone? For example, if a brother or sister in the faith is poorly clothed and hungry and you leave them saying, "Good-bye. I hope you stay warm and have plenty to eat," but you don't provide them with a coat or even a cup of soup, what good is your faith? So then* ***faith that doesn't involve action is phony.*** *But someone might object and say, "One person has faith and another person has works." Go ahead then and prove to me that you have faith without works and I will show you faith by my works as proof that I believe.* (James [Jacob] 2:14–18 TPT, emphasis added)

Then Jesus said, "Come to me, all of you who are weary and carry heavy burdens, and I will give you rest. Take my yoke upon you. Let me teach you, because I am humble and gentle at heart, and you will find rest for your souls. For my yoke is easy to bear, and the burden I give you is light." (Matthew 11:28–30 NLT)

We simply can't give away what we haven't first received, whether that's peace, food, financial provision, or love.

❧

Without the Lord's transforming process, we only have tainted, conditional love to extend to others. Conditional "love" is empty and lackluster with a better chance of gutting someone than ever truly loving that person. We have all watched and read stories about crimes of passion when someone was murdered because the other person "loved her (or him) too much." Most people are sane enough to know that murder has nothing to do with human decency, let alone love. God's love requires the exact opposite. His love compels us to lay down our own lives for others. "So this is my command: Love each other deeply, as much as I have loved you. For the greatest love of all is a love that sacrifices all. And this great love is demonstrated when a person sacrifices his life for his friends" (John 15:12–13 TPT). "But anyone who does not love does not know God, for God is love" (1 John 4:8 NLT).

Characteristics of God's Love

> *Love is large and incredibly patient. Love is gentle and consistently kind to all. It refuses to be jealous when blessing comes to someone else. Love does not brag about one's achievements nor inflate its own importance. Love does not traffic in shame and disrespect, nor selfishly seek its own honor. Love is not easily irritated or quick to take offense. Love joyfully celebrates honesty and finds no delight in what is wrong. Love is a safe place of shelter, for it never stops believing the best for others. Love never takes failure as defeat, for it never gives up. Love never stops loving....* (1 Corinthians 13:4–8 TPT)

Every time I read the passage from 1 Corinthians 13, I am aware that more transformation needs to take place in my own heart. However, I am devoted to staying on my love journey by staying filled with the Holy Spirit and listening to

God's correction and guidance. How about you? Carefully think about every description in that passage and allow the Lord to bring correction and His reality of authentic love to your heart. Would those closest to you describe you as patient and consistently kind? If not, that is a great starting place. Practice yielding to patience and remaining consistently kind in every interaction with every person for 30 days in a row. Then go ahead and reinforce that action by responding in patience and kindness toward others for another 30 days. Responding in love will produce the character of Christ deep within your heart. After that, take another one or two attributes of love to cultivate and become one with.

I'm not suggesting that we can attain this change all on our own with sheer determination. However, I am emphatically saying that no one unintentionally matures in unconditional love or in developing the character of Christ. Maturing and becoming stabilized in God's love can't happen without our complete submission to the Lord and His ways, along with our intentional obedience. None of us have arrived, but we may ask the Lord to teach us how to love others in the same manner and depth. I encourage you to refuse to be deceived by any other definition of love. Pray that your heart will be moved by the perfect, pure love that moves His.

> *True spirituality that is pure in the eyes of our Father God is to make a difference in the lives of the orphans, and widows in their troubles, and to*

> *refuse to be corrupted by the world's values.* (James [Jacob] 1:27 TPT)

Nothing we have received from the Lord was solely for us. Everything we have received from the Lord is for us *and* for everyone around us. From the Lord's perspective, we are all connected in His family.

> *If anyone sees a fellow believer in need and has the means to help him, yet shows no pity and closes his heart against him, how is it even possible that God's love lives in him? Beloved children, our love can't be an abstract theory we only talk about, but a way of life demonstrated through our loving deeds. We know that the truth lives within us because we demonstrate love in action, which will reassure our hearts in his presence.* (1 John 3:17–19 TPT)
>
> *Anyone can say, "I love God," yet have hatred toward another believer. This makes him a phony, because if you don't love a brother or sister, whom you can see, how can you truly love God, whom you can't see? For he has given us this command: whoever loves God must also demonstrate love to others.* (1 John 4:20–21 TPT)

No one unintentionally matures in unconditional love.

❧

Jesus and Mary (Chosen Tween and Teen)

Jesus began learning in the temple at the tender age of 12. That year, after the family's trip to Jerusalem for Passover, He was missing for three days before Mary and Joseph found Him in the temple. "'But why did you need to search?' he asked. 'Didn't you know that I must be in my Father's house?'" (Luke 2:49 NLT) My guess is that everyone reading this book has far surpassed the age of 12; therefore, it is time for all of us to jump in wholeheartedly into learning. The Lord is ready, willing, and well able to instruct us. He is only waiting for our surrendered response of "yes, Lord." Jesus was trained for 30 years for a three-year ministry. In those three years, He packed in miracles, healings, signs, and wonders before His crucifixion and resurrection.

Most biblical scholars agree that Jesus's mother Mary was a teenage virgin when she was chosen to carry Jesus in her womb. In no way could she have felt qualified or equipped for such an important task. Mary was also spiritually pure and mature, and God favored her. Yet, she still had to endure painful accusations from the culture around her. The shame and ridicule that she, her fiancé, and her parents suffered must have been intense.

Perhaps Mary's parents raised her to trust God; we don't know, for they are not even mentioned in the Bible. In other words, this assignment was from God's heart to His teenaged daughter who was found pure and trustworthy before Him. All Mary had was purity, favor, willingness, obedience, and trust in God. Imagine what the Lord can do through us, starting today, if we surrender our hearts and lives in obedient trust. There is no limit to what God can do through us when we consecrate our lives to Him and invite the Spirit of holiness to fall on us and transform us.

> *Gabriel appeared to her and said, "Rejoice, beloved young woman, for the Lord is with you and you are anointed with great favor." Mary was deeply troubled over the words of the angel and bewildered over what this may mean for her. But the angel reassured her, saying, "Do not yield to your fear, Mary, for the Lord has found delight in you and has chosen to surprise you with a wonderful gift. You will become pregnant with a baby boy, and you are to name him Jesus...." Mary said, "But how could this happen? I am still a virgin!" Gabriel answered, "The Spirit of Holiness will fall upon you and almighty God will spread his shadow of power over you in a cloud*

> *of glory! This is why the child born to you will be holy, and he will be called the Son of God. What's more, your aged aunt, Elizabeth, has also become pregnant with a son. The 'barren one' is now in her sixth month. Not one promise from God is empty of power. Nothing is impossible with God!"* (Luke 1:28–31, 34–37 TPT)

Tangible Compassion Testimony

In my mid-20s, I was a junior executive working in marketing and public relations. My coworker provided me with the opportunity to grow in Christ's character on a regular basis. In other words, she grated on my nerves with her mood swings, attitude, insecurities, and futile attempts to control me. In her defense, her mom passed away when she was only 16 years old and her father was an alcoholic. Therefore, she was often irritable, depressed, and existing in survival mode. I leaned on the Lord and His peace while allowing longsuffering to mature within me. Even when it was super challenging, I at least knew to refuse to allow strife and resentment to grow in my heart. I was determined to keep my mouth shut and ignore her passive aggressive antics.

A few years later, she started to feel extremely exhausted and could barely climb one flight of stairs, even though she was only in her late 20s. When her symptoms rapidly worsened, she finally saw a cardiologist. He confirmed that she had a hole in her heart. The cardiologist marveled that she had managed to live with a congenital heart defect for nearly three decades. The moment she was diagnosed, I understood why the adversary had worked so hard to sow discord between us. It became clear to me that the Lord was much more interested in manifesting His tangible compassion to her than in preserving my little feelings.

After her catheterization, our compassionate boss asked me to retrieve my coworker from the hospital and drive her home in lieu of my usual work duties. When I arrived at the hospital, she was not in her hospital room. The Lord instructed me to go to the nurses' station and tell them the truth, as it was obvious that I was most likely not related to her. I told them that her mother was dead and that her father was probably drunk for the day. I told them that I was her friend and the coworker assigned to drive her home. Although it was illegal, they told me that she had been sent to the ICU. This did not make any sense, following a simple catheterization. Open-heart surgery had not even been scheduled until the following week.

I prayed in the Holy Spirit all the way to the ICU. I told the nurses at the station the same story, and they directed me to her room. There was a housekeeper clanging the metal in her room as she cleaned the floor, but my coworker just lay there looking lifeless. I was so overcome with grief that I left and hid in the phone booth to pray in the Holy Spirit, gather my emotions, and call my boss with the update. I was also concerned that if she had awakened and had seen me crying, she would have assumed the worst, since I was rarely emotional. When I returned to her room, she awakened within a few minutes and shared the scary details that had landed her in ICU. During the catheterization procedure, her blood pressure plummeted dangerously low, and she almost died. I stayed with her for hours, providing comfort, encouragement, and prayer. I returned the following day to drive her home.

Her open-heart surgery was postponed an additional week because she was terrified. The night before her surgery, I visited her in the hospital, and she would not let me leave before securing her salvation in Christ. She had been raised in a religious denomination and barely followed their doctrine. She was concerned that since the catheterization nearly killed her, open-heart surgery could definitely end her life. I led her in the salvation prayer, and she accepted Jesus into her heart. I also rebuked the spirit of fear and prayed for supernatural peace and comfort over her. She survived the surgery and healed beautifully. The Lord's tangible compassion showed up for her in many glorious manifestations. I am grateful that the Lord trusted me to assist on earth with His heavenly plan.

The Lord chooses to accomplish His will on earth through people. His will is that we learn His truth and become proficient in ruling and reigning in authority over the enemy. He only needs us to be willing, obedient, available, and listening to Him every day. I have come to realize that there is no season that is all about us or our comforts. The mandate for each one of us is to love the Lord wholeheartedly and to love others as we love ourselves. It's a very tall calling, and it is impossible to complete without total submission to His continuous wisdom, light, and guidance. The wisest, most fulfilling goal of life is to focus on that which pleases the Lord versus us or other people. Every season is a season to mature and gain more understanding of the Lord and His loving ways. Every season is for spiritual growth, gratitude, serving, forgiving, repenting, loving, and living unencumbered for His glory.

There is no season that is all about us or our comforts.

❧

Since God chose you to be the holy people he loves, you must clothe yourselves with tenderhearted mercy, kindness, humility, gentleness, and patience. Make allowance for each other's faults, and forgive anyone who offends you. Remember, the Lord forgave you, so you must forgive others. Above all, clothe yourselves with love, which binds us all together in perfect harmony. And let the peace that comes from Christ rule in your hearts. For as members of one body you are called to live in peace. And always be thankful. Let the message about Christ, in all its richness, fill your lives. Teach and counsel each other with all the wisdom he gives. Sing psalms and hymns and spiritual songs to God with thankful hearts. And whatever you do or say, do it as a representative of the Lord Jesus, giving thanks through him to God the Father. (Colossians 3:12–17 NLT)

Faith without tangible compassion is useless.

Jesus Demonstrated Tangible Compassion

Throughout the Gospels, you will find numerous accounts of Jesus moving with compassion and healing people, restoring life, and feeding multitudes of followers.

Jesus ruined a funeral procession and raised up a widow's only son.

> *When the Lord saw the grieving mother,* ***his heart broke for her****. With great tenderness he said to her, "Please don't cry." Then he stepped up to the coffin and touched it. When the pallbearers came to a halt, Jesus spoke directly to the corpse, "Young man, I say to you, arise and live!" Immediately, the young man moved, sat up, and spoke to those nearby. Jesus presented the son to his mother, alive!* (Luke 7:13–15 TPT, emphasis added)

Then there was the time when Jesus multiplied barley loaves and fish to feed 4,000 men, in addition to their wives and children.

> *Jesus called his disciples to himself and said, "****I care deeply about all these people,*** *for they've already been with me for three days without food. I don't want to send them away fasting or else they may be overcome by weakness on their journey home." The disciples said to him, "Where in the world are we going to find enough food in this desolate place to feed this crowd?" "How many barley loaves do you have?" Jesus asked. "Seven," they replied, "and a few small fish." So he gave the order, "Have the*

> *people sit down on the grass." Then he took the seven loaves and the fish and gave thanks to God. He broke the bread and gave it to his disciples, who then distributed the food to the crowds. When everyone was full and satisfied, they gathered up the leftovers. And from what was once seven loaves and a few fish, they filled seven baskets! There were four thousand men who ate the food Jesus multiplied, and even more including the women and children! After dismissing the crowd, Jesus got into the boat and crossed over to the region of Magdala.* (Matthew 15:32–39 TPT, emphasis added)

Jesus healed every kind of disease and sickness, as no spiritual leader of the time was truly loving and caring for the people. The religious leaders were preoccupied with meaningless rituals and collecting money. They could not have been fully surrendered to God, for they were not providing authentic ministry, which begins with loving and serving people. The Pharisees and Sadducees were quite jealous, irritated, and provoked by Jesus. Jesus was only doing the will of Father God, which is exactly what they were called to do. However, you won't find Jesus searching them out to teach them *anything*. He was focused on implementing the Father's will. The run-ins He had with them only happened as they plotted to catch Him breaking the law so that they could accuse Him. Instead of loving, serving, and ministering to people, they loved the attention they received, for their own selfish reasons. Their outrageous jealousy and greed caused them to collaborate with evil to have Jesus crucified.

> *Jesus walked throughout the region with the joyful message of God's kingdom realm. He taught in their meeting houses, and wherever he went he demonstrated God's power by healing every kind of disease and illness. When he saw the vast crowds of people, Jesus' heart was deeply moved with compassion, because they seemed weary and helpless, like wandering sheep without a shepherd. He turned to his disciples and said, "The harvest is huge and ripe! But there are not enough harvesters to bring it all in."* (Matthew 9:35–37 TPT)

Jesus's compassion also showed up tangibly when He healed a woman who had been crippled for nearly two decades.

> *He encountered a seriously handicapped woman. She was crippled and had been doubled over for eighteen years. Her condition was caused by a demonic spirit of bondage that had left her unable to stand up straight. When Jesus saw her condition, he called her to him and gently laid his hands on her. Then he said, "Dear woman, you*

> *are free. I release you forever from this crippling spirit." Instantly she stood straight and tall and overflowed with glorious praise to God!* (Luke 13:11–13 TPT)

In another demonstration of compassion, Jesus's heart was moved to help a woman from outside of the country He was sent to minister in, which was Israel. This is a great reminder to us to remain tuned in to the Father's heart even after receiving the initial assignment. We must be careful not to run full speed ahead as if God downloaded every single detail of the assignment. Honestly, it's not wise to ever unplug from His wisdom. I'm sure God's voice led this foreign woman to seek Jesus's help to heal her daughter. She pushed past her fear and the criticism of the crowd and focused on receiving a miracle for her daughter who was being tormented by a demon. She remained humble and tenacious even when she was referred to as a dog. She stayed in a place of faith and trust in the Lord, which granted access to her daughter's miracle. She wasn't allowing her pride, ego, or hurt feelings to get in the way of her daughter's miracle. Surely the adversary was there screaming at her to become offended by Jesus's words. But she did not have time to be offended, as that would have proven deadly. Tangible compassion met her right there.

> *He encountered there a Canaanite woman who shouted out to him, "Lord, Son of David, show mercy to me! My daughter is horribly afflicted by a demon that torments her." But Jesus never answered her. So his disciples said to him, "Why do you ignore this woman who is crying out to us?" Jesus said, "I've only been sent to the lost sheep of Israel." But she came and bowed down before him and said, "Lord, help me!" Jesus responded, "It's not right for a man to take bread from his children and throw it out to the dogs." "You're right, Lord," she replied. "But even puppies get to eat the crumbs that fall from the prince's table." Then Jesus answered her, "Dear woman,* ***your faith is strong!*** *What you desire will be done for you."* ***And at that very moment, her daughter was instantly set free from demonic torment.*** (Matthew 15:22–28 TPT, emphasis added)

This woman passed the offense test with flying colors! (See Psalm 119:165.)

For many years I was challenged to understand what I perceived as the Lord's "rude" words to the woman who desperately needed His help. However, because I knew the Lord's loving and compassionate nature, I put my lack of understanding to the side and continued to trust Him and

His unconditional love. The need to adjust is always on our end whenever we don't understand something found in the Word of God. It's an invitation to keep studying and asking the Holy Spirit for more revelation and understanding. When we don't understand something is not the time to accuse the Lord of anything, nor is it the time to assume that we are more wise, loving, and kind than He is! I never recommend following such arrogant, ego-driven, prideful, foolish thinking. I am thankful for the Holy Spirit's clarification, which brings greater understanding. I also appreciate the wise biblical teachers who have shared their revelations. However, even when we are taught by the most studious teachers, their insights need to bear witness with the Holy Spirit on the inside of us before we take in their teaching as truth. That being said, please verify the wisdom found in these pages with the Holy Spirit inside you. Please don't just run it by your intellect.

Jesus did many other loving, compassionate, miraculous things to help people. "...If they were all written down, I suppose the whole world could not contain the books that would be written" (John 21:25 NLT).

Compassion Meditation

The Father's heart and the Bible are aligned. Therefore, the more we study the Word of God and follow Christ's compassionate example, the more our hearts will be in sync with the Father's heart, Here are some scriptures you can meditate on to expand your process of implementing compassion into your everyday life.

> *Learn to do good. Seek justice. Help the oppressed. Defend the cause of orphans. Fight for the rights of widows.* (Isaiah 1:17 NLT)
>
> *We will show mercy to the poor and not miss an opportunity to do acts of kindness for others, for these are the true sacrifices that delight God's heart.* (Hebrews 13:16 TPT)
>
> *You must each decide in your heart how much to give. And don't give reluctantly or in response to pressure. "For God loves a person who gives cheerfully." And God will generously provide all you need. Then you will always have everything you need and plenty left over to share with others. As the Scriptures say, "They share freely and give generously to the poor. Their good deeds will be remembered forever." For God is the one who provides seed for the farmer and then bread to eat. In the same way, he will provide and increase your resources and then produce a great harvest of generosity in you. Yes, you will be enriched in every way so that you can always be generous. And when*

we take your gifts to those who need them, they will thank God. (2 Corinthians 9:7–11 NLT)

"I had no place to stay, and you refused to take me in as your guest. When you saw me poorly clothed, you closed your hearts and did not clothe me. When you saw that I was sick, you didn't lift a finger to help me, and when I was imprisoned, you never came to visit me." And then those on his left will say, "Lord, when did we see you hungry or thirsty and not give you food and something to drink? When did we see you homeless, or poorly clothed? When did we see you sick and not help you, or in prison and not visit you?" Then he will answer them, "Don't you know? When you refused to help one of the least important among these my little ones, my true brothers and sisters, you refused to help and honor me." (Matthew 25:43–45 TPT)

Practical Life Application

- Refuse to be corrupted by the culture or its definition of love. (See James 1:27.)
- Exchange your thoughts, opinions, and ways for God's.
- Pursue truth and holiness. (See Hebrews 12:14.)

- Practice walking in the Spirit versus by the dictates of your mind or flesh.
- As you're getting dressed in the morning, remember to clothe yourself with love, tenderhearted mercy, kindness, humility, gentleness, and patience.
- Practice forgiving and believing the best about every person.
- Practice yielding to patience and kindness in the middle of annoyance.
- Demonstrate your faith with tangible compassion toward yourself and others.
- Find people to love and serve, especially widows and orphans. (See James 1:27.)
- Ask the Lord every day if there's someone on His heart whom you can help.
- Remember Jesus's prayer for us: "Your Word is truth! So make them holy by the truth" (John 17:17 TPT).

Chapter 2

Heaven's Reality on Earth

Before anyone can master loving and serving others well, he or she must be willing to let go of hindering mindsets. It takes courage to take an honest look at your roadmap to life. It is even more challenging when your life is successful, as defined by American culture. However, if, at the core of your being, you welcome being stretched by God and want to enjoy more of the benefits of Heaven in everyday life, then this journey is for you.

The first step leads you into the compassionate arms of *truth*. I am not speaking of my truth, as that would be as flawed as yours. I am speaking of the wisdom and truth that come from a revelation of who Jesus is (John 14:6) and from the Spirit of truth versus an intellectual, humanistic opinion. Absolute truth leads to reservoirs of peace that quiet your mind and steady your feet. The only way to discern absolute truth is by drawing close to and accepting the Truth

(Jesus) and by receiving revelation from the Spirit of truth (the Holy Spirit).

> *Jesus said to him, I am the Way and the Truth and the Life; no one comes to the Father except by (through) Me.* (John 14:6 AMPC)
>
> *When the Spirit of truth comes, he will guide you into all truth. He will not speak on his own but will tell you what he has heard. He will tell you about the future. He will bring me glory by telling you whatever he receives from me. All that belongs to the Father is mine; this is why I said, "The Spirit will tell you whatever he receives from me."* (John 16:13–15 NLT)

Thayer's defines truth as, objectively, "what is true in any matter under consideration...in *reality*..." and, subjectively, "that candor of mind which is free from affection, pretense, simulation, falsehood, deceit."[1] Deception is running rampant, and there are many skillful liars vying for your attention. Believing the enemy's lies or your own is very costly. "There is a way which seems right to a man and appears straight before him, but at the end of it is the way of death" (Proverbs 14:12 AMPC).

I encourage you to challenge your belief systems, thoughts, mindsets, and choices. Your willingness to become honest about what was life-giving for you and what has stolen from you, brings your divine turnaround closer. This is not an invitation to rev up negative self-talk or pummel yourself with criticism. Trust me, that will not be helpful or constructive. However, you will absolutely need a made-up mind about whose "truth" you will follow and the direction in which you are moving forward. Jesus has provided access into the loving heart of the one true and living God. Having completed all of the heavy lifting, He longs to restore you to favor with your heavenly Father. Your part is to repent, forgive, and ask God for His help and His wisdom. I too came to the end of myself; I humbled myself and asked for His grace, help, forgiveness, and full salvation as a lifestyle.

> *If we [freely] admit that we have sinned and confess our sins, He is faithful and just (true to His own nature and promises) and will forgive our sins [dismiss our lawlessness] and [continuously] cleanse us from all unrighteousness [everything not in conformity to His will in purpose, thought, and action]. If we say (claim) we have not sinned, we contradict His Word and make Him out to be false and a liar, and His Word is not in us [the divine message of the Gospel is not in our hearts].* (1 John 1:9–10 AMPC)

The only way to discern absolute truth is by drawing close to and accepting the Truth (Jesus) and by receiving revelation from the Spirit of truth (the Holy Spirit).

❧

Restored Favor

A truth that's worth internalizing is that God favors us. Human beings have had God's heart since conception. Out of everything He created, people are the only beings created in His image and given full access to every blessing He has. We are the only ones He calls His children and the only ones who are redeemable. We have been invited into a deep relationship with the Lord to receive unconditional love and unlimited blessings as we fulfill our destiny.

> *Whatever is good and perfect is a gift coming down to us from God our Father, who created all the lights in the heavens. He never changes or casts a shifting shadow. He chose to give birth to us by giving us his true word. And we, out of all creation, became his prized possession.* (James 1:17–18 NLT)

Wherever our lives are incongruent with His favor reveals the need for an adjustment on our end. In return, He desires a loving relationship with us so we may enjoy Heaven on earth and share in the riches of His lovingkindness.

Father God never intended for us to only hear about His goodness and favor. He wants us to experience every manifestation of His compassion in tangible, measurable ways. His perfect will is that our minds experience palpable peace and joy right in the middle of a problem. If you are wondering how that is even possible, please read on. The good news is that peace is not the absence of a problem; rather, it is found and experienced within the Lord's presence. "You will show me the path of life; in Your presence is fullness of joy, at Your right hand there are pleasures forevermore" (Psalm 16:11 AMPC).

The Power of Humility

Those who are truly wise value humility. They understand that life is much harder when God Himself is opposing, resisting, and pushing them back.

> *And he gives grace generously. As the Scriptures say, "God opposes the proud but gives grace to the humble." So humble yourselves before God. Resist the devil, and he will flee from you. Come close to*

> *God, and God will come close to you. Wash your hands, you sinners; purify your hearts, for your loyalty is divided between God and the world.* (James 4:6–8 NLT)

Humility is the shortcut to receiving the Lord's wisdom and help. The Lord never removes our free will, not even to keep us from destroying our relationships and lives or spending eternity in hell. It's our choice to make. However, hell was never intended for people; it was prepared solely for the fallen angels. (See Matthew 25:41.)

Humility is the shortcut to freedom.

❧

Those whom the culture perceives and promotes as powerful icons are rarely known for humility. However, I see humility as a powerful secret weapon of mass destruction. The first thing it annihilates is our pride and arrogance, which no one finds attractive.

Where there's conflict, humility serves to disarm people. It just takes the fight out of the fight. Once we have chosen humility as our mode of operation, repentance and forgiveness are much easier to attain. Repentance and forgiveness keep our hearts from becoming hardened and log-jammed with pain and resentment. Please do not hold yourself hostage by waiting for anyone to admit to any offense. Do not wait for others to ask for your forgiveness. Go ahead and forgive them, pray for them, bless them, and take the shortcut to your freedom. Rather than take offense, gift your mind and heart with immediate access to supernatural peace. "There is such a *great peace* and well-being that comes to the lovers of your Word, and they will *never be offended*" (Psalm 119:165 TPT, emphasis added).

A humble heart is postured to receive sound wisdom and understanding, which the Lord is eager to supply upon request.

> *And if anyone longs to be wise, ask God for wisdom and he will give it! He won't see your lack of wisdom as an opportunity to scold you over your failures but he will overwhelm your failures with his generous grace. Just make sure you ask empowered by confident faith without doubting that you will receive. For the ambivalent person believes one minute and doubts the next. Being undecided makes you become like the rough seas driven and tossed by the wind. You're up one minute and tossed down the next. When you are half-hearted and wavering it leaves you unstable. Can you really expect to receive anything from the Lord when you're in that condition?* (James [Jacob] 1:5–8 TPT)

Take an Inventory

The humble are peaceful on the inside. They are not agitated, moody, complaining, or combative. Their focus is on listening attentively for the Lord's guidance. They are living in the Spirit, preoccupied with prayer and gratitude, and cannot imagine blaming God for anything. They fully understand and believe that it's the humble who receive the help. "Humble yourselves [feeling very insignificant] in the presence of the Lord, and He will exalt you [He will lift you up and make your lives significant]" (James 4:10 AMPC).

Imagine how choosing to walk in humility will greatly impact your inner dialogue. It helps your mind stop arguing and submit to transformation by absolute truth. Once the debate ends, your inner dialogue can become reprogrammed by sound wisdom and prudence. Prudence is defined by *Merriam-Webster* as "the ability to govern and discipline oneself by use of reason...shrewdness in the management of affairs, skill and good judgment in the use of resources, caution or circumspection as to danger or risk."[2]

The humble get the help.

Take an honest inventory of your thoughts and choices and label each one as humble or arrogant, healthy or unhealthy, good or evil, and wise or foolish. In a few short hours, you may be appalled by the amount of toxic thoughts that have been feeding you consciously and subconsciously. A sabotaging inner dialogue is very costly since it's the very gateway the adversary uses to traffic lies, fear, and torment to you. Your own blood and brain chemistry are the first to drink its poison, which then contaminates your entire body, relationships, and life.

A sabotaging inner dialogue is very costly since it's the very gateway the adversary uses to traffic lies, fear, and torment to you.

❧

Resiliency in Christ

Your life can begin to trend upward starting today. Resiliency requires your decision to change whatever is necessary to fully recover from every devastation. The Father, Jesus, and the Holy Spirit are ready, willing, and well able to help you bounce back and awaken to wholeness and holiness. I ask the Lord for help, mercy, grace, and forgiveness every day. Before your eyes open in the morning, God's new and tender mercies are waiting for you!

> *The faithful love of the LORD never ends! His mercies never cease. Great is his faithfulness; his mercies begin afresh each morning. I say to myself, "The LORD is my inheritance; therefore, I will hope in him!" The LORD is good to those who depend on him, to those who search for him. So it is good to wait quietly for salvation from the LORD. And it is good for people to submit at an early age to the yoke of his discipline.* (Lamentations 3:22–27 NLT)

Merriam-Webster defines resiliency as "an ability to recover from or adjust easily to adversity or change."[3] Resiliency fueled by the Spirit of truth empowers us to overcome all adversity. The apostle Paul says it this way:

> *I know what it means to lack, and I know what it means to experience overwhelming abundance. For I'm trained in the secret of overcoming all things, whether in fullness or in hunger. And I find that the strength of Christ's explosive power infuses me to conquer every difficulty.* (Philippians 4:12–13 TPT)

We have all suffered pain, loss, trauma, and devastation, which the enemy hopes to use to wound and trap us for even decades. However, it is not the height, depth, or quantity of tragedies that determine our outcome; rather, it is our submission to and cooperation with the Lord that matter most. My prayer is that every reader is committed to finding the most healthy and effective way through and out of crisis with peace and joy intact. As previously mentioned, I am not one who values worthless theories and philosophies. I only value tried and true, sound wisdom. Please rest assured that the strategies I teach align with biblical truths that contain more than enough power to completely transform your life. Accept your invitation into an authentic relationship with the Lord to receive unconditional love and unlimited blessings. Truly, there is nothing too hard for God. (See Luke 1:37.)

The Perils of Religion

It will serve you well to know whether your religion is pure, healthy, and life-giving or just a religious system that has you spinning your wheels in religious activity. Theory, hype, and powerless religion all fail miserably.

True spirituality is defined by the Spirit of truth and by the Word of God. It is not defined by me, you, your favorite guru, or a corrupted culture. "True spirituality that is pure in the eyes of our Father God is to make a difference in the lives of the orphans, and widows in their troubles, and to refuse to be corrupted by the world's values" (James [Jacob] 1:27 TPT).

Stale, lifeless, powerless, man-made religious systems are predictively lacking in compassion. They simply won't provide tangible help when a crisis has you by the throat. When trouble comes and religious people and religious systems fail, many blame God; however, He is the only one who *can't* fail.

> *He alone is my safe place; his wraparound presence always protects me. For he is my champion defender; there's no risk of failure with God. So why would I let worry paralyze me, even when troubles multiply around me?* (Psalm 62:2 TPT)

I too have had to let go of human reasoning, a bossy ego, and powerless religious paradigms. The Lord is the only steady foundation who anchors us in His faithful love and merciful kindness. My pursuit is to love the Lord and His truth wholeheartedly and to love others as myself. My focus is on continuing to mature in Christlike character and to live ready to love and serve as the Lord leads.

> *Jesus answered him, "'Love the Lord your God with every passion of your heart, with all the energy of your being, and with every thought that is within*

> *you.' This is the great and supreme commandment. And the second is like it in importance: 'You must love your friend in the same way you love yourself.'"* (Matthew 22:37–39 TPT)

For those who assume they are exempt from the snares of religion just because they label themselves as atheists or agnostics, please hear my heart: you are not unscathed. Perhaps your god is money, intellect, your job, pride, ego, another person, or yourself. Everyone is paying homage to something or someone, whether knowingly or blindly in enslavement. We were created to experience the Lord's glory, and we were created for His glory.

> *Bring me everyone who is called by my name, the ones I created to experience my glory. I myself formed them to be who they are and made them for my glory. Lead out those who have eyes but are blind, those who have ears but are deaf.* (Isaiah 43:7–8 TPT)

Creator God does not need anyone's agreement or approval to be God. He is God alone. The truth is, we were created to enjoy a loving, thriving relationship with Him that yields unlimited benefits. Unlimited wisdom, help, and power are available to anyone who invites His Son Jesus into his or her life as Lord and Savior.

Don't you realize that grace frees you to choose your own master? But choose carefully, for you surrender yourself to become a servant—bound to the one you choose to obey. If you choose to love sin, it will become your master, and it will own you and reward you with death. But if you choose to love and obey God, he will lead you into perfect righteousness. And thanks be to God, for in the past you were servants of sin, but now your obedience is heart deep, and your life is being molded by truth through the teaching you are devoted to. (Romans 6:16–17 TPT)

The Lord is the only steady foundation who anchors us with His faithful love and merciful kindness.

❧

Fortunately, God backs up His truth and promises with unconditional love and unlimited power and provision. He is perfectly and completely in love with us. Motivated by perfect love, He chose to give us a free will. Perfect love honors our free will, even when we choose to use it to wall Him out. He's in love, and we cannot change it, for God *is* love.

But anyone who does not love does not know God, for God is love. God showed how much he loved us by sending his one and only Son into the world so that we might have eternal life through him. ... We know how much God loves us, and we have put our trust in his love. God is love, and all who live in love live in God, and God lives in them. (1 John 4:8–9, 16 NLT)

Yahweh appeared to me from another realm and said, "I have deeply loved you with a forever-love; that is why I have been so patient and kind to draw you to my heart." (Jeremiah 31:3 TPT)

Practical Life Application

- Choose God; He loves you. "God did not send his Son into the world to judge and condemn the world, but to be its Savior and rescue it!" (John 3:17 TPT) If you have not already accepted Jesus as your Savior, pray this prayer right now: "Lord Jesus, I believe that I am a sinner in need of a Savior. I ask You to be my Savior, and I invite You into my heart. Thank You for going to the cross, redeeming me, and washing me from sin with Your blood. Thank You that I am now a child of the Father! In Jesus's name, amen."

- Reject offense and resentment. Pray this instead: "Father, I choose to forgive [insert name]. I refuse to harbor bitterness and anger against him (or her). I release [insert name] to You. I ask You to encounter him (or her) by Your love and to bless him (or her) with Your wisdom, light, and truth. Thank You, Lord, that I am free, and I ask You to bring freedom to [insert name], in the mighty name of Jesus. Amen!"
- Reserve time to worship God.
- Ask God to teach you about Himself and His ways.
- Pray every day about everything.

> "The Spirit wants you to honor and discern the boundaries and then you can learn and just walk a straight line."
>
> —Dr. Kevin Zadai

Chapter 3

Accessible Peace and Joy

There are a few things I am addicted to. By "addicted," I mean having an insatiable desire. They are, in order of desire, the manifested presence and glory of God, friendship with Jesus, wisdom, peace, joy, clean food/water, and seven and a half to nine hours of uninterrupted, sweet sleep. All day, every day, regardless of the chaos that may have been unleashed, peace, joy, and sweet sleep are still the portions that God has for us. Dr. Daniel Amen, currently the leading psychiatrist in the world, has stated that "while you're snoozing, your brain is hard at work, performing some very critical functions necessary to keep it operating at optimal levels. For example, during sleep, your brain cleans or washes itself by eliminating cellular debris and toxins that build up during the day (basically taking out the neural trash), consolidates learning and memory, and prepares for the next day."[1] Having learned this truth, not only am

I maintaining healthy sleeping habits, but I also encourage everyone to cultivate great sleeping habits. You may believe that you are fully rejuvenated after only five or six hours of sleep. However, it's simply a familiar habit that doesn't provide adequate time for your brain and body to repair itself. Fear and worry are the antithesis to sound sleep. From this moment on, I pray that you will only be overwhelmed by God's love and never again become overwhelmed by fear. One of my favorite promises regarding sleep is this: "You will sleep like a baby, safe and sound—your rest will be sweet and secure" (Proverbs 3:24 TPT).

> *Yahweh, you alone are my inheritance. You are my prize, my pleasure, and my portion. You hold my destiny and its timing in your hands. Your pleasant path leads me to pleasant places. I'm overwhelmed by the privileges that come with following you! The way you counsel me makes me praise you more, for your whispers in the night give me wisdom, showing me what to do next. Because I set you, Yahweh, always close to me, my confidence will never be weakened, for I experience your wraparound presence every moment.* (Psalm 16:5–8 TPT)

Everyone goes through trouble, trials, and wilderness seasons. The key to hope is staying connected to the Lord to receive help and strength every step of the way. His will is that we remain healthy and unencumbered. His will is that we overcome adversity instead of becoming casualties of traumatic life events. "You will keep in perfect peace all who trust in you, all whose thoughts are fixed on you! Trust in the LORD always, for the LORD GOD is the eternal Rock" (Isaiah 26:3–4 NLT). "I stop to praise you seven times a day, all because your ways are perfect! There is such a great peace and well-being that comes to the lovers of your Word, and they will never be offended" (Psalm 119:164–165 TPT).

From this moment on, I pray that you will only be overwhelmed by God's love and never again be overwhelmed by fear.

There is only one living God who created all that exists. Every other god is an idol and a misinformed fixation or figment of someone's strange imagination. That is the truth, which is higher and supersedes facts. Please remember that facts, by definition, are based on observation. Just because a person has not observed, perceived, or experienced God and His truth does not change His existence or true reality. For example, God created gravity long before it was observed and experienced by humans and long before

Isaac Newton was born to discover the laws of gravity and motion. "YAHWEH says, 'You are my witnesses, my chosen servants. I chose you in order that you would know me intimately, believe me always, and fully understand that I am the only God. There was no god before me, and there will be no other god after me'" (Isaiah 43:10 TPT). "The words of YAHWEH, Israel's true King and Kinsman-Redeemer, YAHWEH, Commander of Angel Armies, says: 'I am the Beginning and I am the Ending, and I am the only God there is'" (Isaiah 44:6 TPT).

When Father God created us, He gave us a free will, even though He knew we would use it to choose poorly. His plan of salvation and redemption—that Jesus would be crucified—was decided *before* He formed the earth, long before people were created.

> *For you know that God paid a ransom to save you from the empty life you inherited from your ancestors. And it was not paid with mere gold or silver, which lose their value. It was the precious blood of Christ, the sinless, spotless Lamb of God. God chose him as your ransom long before the world began, but now in these last days he has been revealed for your sake.* (1 Peter 1:18–20 NLT)

Holy Connection

A few years ago, I had a vision of an umbilical cord that was attached to my heart. The other end extended into the heavens and connected to God's heart. I believe the Lord was encouraging me through this vision to live connected in fellowship with Him. He was also reassuring me that He was constantly sustaining me. "Behold, God is my helper; the Lord is the sustainer of my soul" (Psalm 54:4 NASB 1995). Our part is to maintain a healthy relationship with the Father, Jesus, and the Holy Spirit. It's also on us to pray, repent, and forgive as a lifestyle. Years ago, I heard the Lord say, "*Many of My loved ones are caught up in drama when I intended for them to enjoy musicals instead.*"

I encourage you to practice responding to bad news by praying and trusting God for the divine turnaround. Another healthy response is to sing a spontaneous, thankful song to the Lord. Of course, I am not suggesting that anyone be thankful *for* the problem, but rather to remain thankful for the faithful goodness of God *in spite of* the problem. You may not feel like singing a thankful song, but would you prefer feeling agitated and anxious? Sometimes making a change is as simple as choosing to have another great day of resting in the faithfulness of God by not allowing negative thoughts to run rampant. He is with you and for you, and He is able to carry you through every circumstance. So please do not sing about the problem and how afraid you are. For those who insist on doing so, please keep all whining lyrics short and instead elaborate on the faithfulness of God. In other words, focus your heart-song on exalting God, not the problem.

Use your creativity, imagination, and vocal cords to make melodies in your heart to the Lord. Responding with creativity is more helpful and more rewarding than worrying. Since people were made in the image of God who created all that exists, I believe everyone is creative, whether people have explored and discovered their creativity or not.

George Land developed a creativity test which was used to select the most innovative engineers and scientists to work for NASA. The assessment was successful, and he decided to try it on children. "What we have concluded," wrote Land, "is that non-creative behavior is learned." Land's conclusion is based on his research which he conducted in 1968. The research study tested the creativity of 1,600 children ranging in ages from three to five years old. He later re-tested the same children at 10 years, and again at 15 years of age. The test results:

- **98%** (5 years old)
- **30%** (10 years old)
- **12%** (15 years old)
- **2%** (280,000 adults)"[2]

You still have creativity. Release it!

Every psalm in the book of Psalms are songs that were mostly written and sung by David, who became king. I am well aware that David sang the blues a bit before his glorious turnaround lyrics; however, I do not recommend doing so. He also had a concubine when he became king, another choice that I cannot recommend. I am not throwing David under the proverbial bus here, as I know that he was a man after God's heart. However, I am emphatically stating that *King Jesus* is my ideal example, not David or any other person.

Instead of worrying, use your creativity, imagination, and vocal cords to make melodies in your heart to the Lord.

❧

So be careful how you live. Don't live like fools, but like those who are wise. Make the most of every opportunity in these evil days. Don't act thoughtlessly, but understand what the Lord wants you to do. Don't be drunk with wine, because that will ruin your life. Instead, be filled with the Holy Spirit, singing psalms and hymns and spiritual

> *songs among yourselves, and making music to the Lord in your hearts. And give thanks for everything to God the Father in the name of our Lord Jesus Christ.* (Ephesians 5:15–20 NLT)

Including the names of God and referring to the blood of Jesus in your lyrics is a surefire way to send the enemy into panic as he flees in seven directions! (See Deuteronomy 28:7.) The enemy is not afraid of negative, complaining lyrics or prayers about the problem. The enemy's strategy is to bombard you with fear, hoping you give up—preferably in a fetal position for hours and even decades. The demonic vibration will swarm in and try to suck you into its vortex of fear. On the other hand, the enemy is horrified when we respond in confident prayer, gratitude, and worship to God. The Lord God, strong and mighty, will be there drawing you with lovingkindness and tender mercies; He will be there with a way of escape into His loving comfort with illogical peace.

> *We all experience times of testing, which is normal for every human being. But God will be faithful to you. He will screen and filter the severity, nature, and timing of every test or trial you face so that you can bear it. And each test is an opportunity to trust him more, for along with every trial God has provided for you a way of escape that will bring you out of it victoriously.* (1 Corinthians 10:13 TPT)

Long ago the LORD said to Israel: "I have loved you, my people, with an everlasting love. With unfailing love I have drawn you to myself." (Jeremiah 31:3 NLT)

The Lord chose to reveal Himself to Israel first; however, all believers have the same rock-solid agreement and unconditional love from God. In fact, we have an even better covenant with God sealed by the blood of Jesus.

Another stellar response to fear-provoking news is to pray in the Holy Spirit. I understand how counterintuitive this may sound, especially if your mind has not been transformed and your inner dialogue has yet to be reprogrammed to work for you and not against you. However, I have practiced receiving God's perfect love instead of reacting in fear for decades through many crises, and I assure you that praying in the Spirit is highly effective.

Love never brings fear, for fear is always related to punishment. But love's perfection drives the fear of punishment far from our hearts. Whoever walks constantly afraid of punishment has not reached love's perfection. Our love for others is our grateful response to the love God first demonstrated to us. (1 John 4:18–19 TPT)

Praying in the Spirit is highly effective.

Personal Testimony

I had taken my marital vows for better or for worse very seriously, and I was willing to grow old with my husband. However, 25 years into our marriage, his midlife crisis led him further away from Christ's standards and into adultery. Dulled by escapism, he strayed away from his faith and destiny, dropped his spiritual guard, and allowed the dogs and demons in to kill, steal, and destroy. When the Lord exposed his adultery, he was not willing to admit the sin, let alone repent and accept God's healing and deliverance. Instead, he lied and denied everything and chose to collaborate with pride. He refused the invitation for pastoral and secular counseling. Using his God-given free will, he chose to run away and hide in shame in the cesspool he had created with a woman who was also cheating on her husband. He ignored his covenant with God, along with his covenant of marriage, bowing instead to idolatry and double adultery.

God Is My Husband

> *For your Maker is your Husband—the Lord of hosts is His name—and the Holy One of Israel is your Redeemer; the God of the whole earth He is called.* (Isaiah 54:5 AMPC)
>
> *I will return her vineyards to her and transform the Valley of Trouble into a gateway of hope. She will give herself to me there, as she did long ago when she was young, when I freed her from her captivity in Egypt.* (Hosea 2:15 NLT)

I connected with God with everything in me, for I desperately needed His help through the dark season of divorce. In the natural realm, things looked bleak rather quickly as my now ex-husband stopped paying the mortgage and my home went into foreclosure. As I was approaching 90 days into the crisis of divorce, I found myself amid an intense, spiritual battle. Of course, I had continued to do everything I knew to do. I was feeding my spirit, praying in English and in the Holy Spirit, repenting, forgiving, and worshiping along with worship music, yet the second I stopped, many tormenting thoughts from the enemy invaded my mind. Within an hour, I slammed my hand down on the kitchen counter and went to my keyboard. I picked out four chords and began worshiping God about who He was to me, at that very moment. The words of my spontaneous and heartfelt worship were these:

(Chorus)
God, You're my Sustainer
You're the One I rely on
The God who is stronger
Stronger than anything,
That I'll face, in my life.
(God, yes, You are!)
You're my strong Tower
You're the Lord my Provider
My amazing Daddy God
You are my King
And my steadfast place

I sang this over and over and over to the Lord. Eventually two verses rose up from within me. The lyrics were as follows:

(Verse one)
Nothing I'm facing has taken You by surprise.
Lord, You've known all things
Long before the sun could rise.
And You've gone before me,
To light the way of my path
Still You walk beside me even now.

(Verse two)
You have prepared me
For this journey I'm on.
Still there are times,
I am carried in Your loving arms.
I'm going straight through
Straight through to the other side.
"No more delay"
God, I hear You say
Right on time!

Then I'd go back to the chorus:

(Chorus)
You're my Sustainer
You're the One I rely on
The God who is stronger
Stronger than anything,
That I'll face, in my life.
(God, yes, You are!)
You're my strong Tower
You're the Lord my Provider
My amazing Daddy God
You are my King
And my steadfast place[3]

Well, I am happy to testify that perfect Love came running to rescue me! To this day, I have no idea whether I was on my keyboard for 45 minutes or 90 minutes. All I know is that my entire being and physical home were enveloped in what I can only describe as a blissful, holy hush. Surely. the very shalom of God came rushing in, filling me with perfect peace and sending the enemy running in terror in seven directions! "The Lord shall cause your enemies who rise up against you to be defeated before your face; they shall come out against you one way and flee before you seven ways" (Deuteronomy 28:7 AMPC).

What the enemy had planned to use to overwhelm me turned into a catalyst for a peaceful day of victory! Hallelujah! I had never referred to God as my Sustainer before, and the enemy tried to immediately distract me by launching the thought that "sustainer" wasn't even in the Bible. But, of course, the enemy is a liar! I am glad I ignored the enemy and kept right on worshiping. Afterwards I searched my concordance and found this verse: "Cast your burden on the Lord [releasing the weight of it] and He will *sustain* you; He will never allow the [consistently] righteous to be moved (made to slip, fall, or fail)" (Psalm 55:22 AMPC, emphasis added).

I relied on the Lord for all three years of my separation and divorce process. I trusted the Lord one day at a time and worshiped Him in the waiting. My home remained in foreclosure, and part of the roof actually collapsed during this timeframe. There were days when I prophetically called my house out of foreclosure and called myself as the sole owner of the house. I did not have relatives in the state of New Jersey, but I did have a faithful, loving God, who I am sure picked me up and carried me many days. I refused to worry through all of the unknowns, as that would have wreaked havoc on every system in my body and destroyed the peace and sleep I desperately needed. I was now trusting the same Spirit of counsel that the Lord had poured through me into others who were in crisis. I would've loved having a wise, stable counselor, but I could not find one I trusted. Had I found one, I'm sure the Lord would have provided the means to pay for his or her time. Like King David, I encouraged myself in the Lord all day, every day. (See 1 Samuel 30:6b.)

Abasing and Abounding

There were far too many times when I went without things I had previously seen as necessities. I remember standing in the grocery store, thinking of how I could make one roast chicken last for a week. I also convinced myself that I really did not need paper towels and other nonessentials. I was very thankful that I was able to send my daughter's weekly stipend, as she was in college at the time.

Although car brakes are very essential, I could not afford to replace the brake pads. Having no other means of transportation, I avoided the highway when I absolutely needed to drive because I was stopping on the rotors for months, once the brake pads were completely worn out.

Part of my roof also collapsed during this time, as mentioned earlier. Immediately the enemy taunted me that snakes would be able to get into my home, since I have a lot of trees. I remember prophetically applying the blood of Jesus and forbidding anything to crawl through the damaged area. I also thanked God for assigning angels to hold up the roof until I could get it fixed. The Holy Spirit reminded me of Paul's words in his letter to the Philippians, and I decided it was an opportune season to learn how to keep my peace and joy while remaining thankful for what I had.

My now ex-husband filed for divorce about eight months after separating, under New Jersey's "we don't care" count of irreconcilable differences. I forgave him and released him, countering with a two-count motion of adultery and irreconcilable differences. He fought the adultery count until the very end. During the last half hour of our marriage, right in the courtroom, the fear of the Lord caused him to accept that his adultery and adulteress would be reflected in court records. As a Christian marriage counselor, it was important that no one could assume I had taken my marital vows lightly or that I believed irreconcilable differences were an acceptable, biblical reason to divorce.

The divorce finally ended, and I was awarded my home in the settlement. Three weeks beforehand, the Lord reminded me of specific words in a prophetic word I received 22 years earlier when He had said, "And I will provide a homeland for you, planting you in a secure place where they will never be disturbed. Evil nations won't oppress you as they've done in the past" (2 Samuel 7:10 NLT, slightly paraphrased and personalized).

I threw my hands up in heartfelt gratitude to God, believing that the timing of His reminder meant that I would keep my home in the settlement! In the state of New Jersey, divorce is just math. The lower salary is subtracted from the top salary, and the remaining balance is divided by three. One third goes to each person and the last third goes to taxes. Because I had spent 15 years as a housewife raising our precious daughter, his income was three times higher than mine. The fact that I was married more than 25 years meant that he would owe me alimony until he was physically retired. My attorney told me to put my home up for sale to split the equity. However, in exchange for permanent alimony, I heard the Lord's instruction to take only ten years of alimony in exchange for the house and all of the equity in the house. In the natural, that would potentially flush hundreds of thousands of dollars over time. I trusted the wisdom of the Lord. It was a deal he could not refuse, for he was a writer and could easily write well into his 80s. Thank God for His wisdom and counsel, as my ex-husband ended up losing his job of more than 30 years. Instead of paying me out with his severance package, he spent it and weaseled out of alimony in less than six years. I petitioned the court to force payment, to no avail. I forgave him, as well as the family court of New Jersey, and I bless him upon every remembrance. I continue to rest assured of the Lord's provision.

The Lord continues to bless the counseling ministry that He called me to establish and serve in. He fills my schedule with those who need help every week, as I have no other source of income. I could never have imagined that serving others in a counseling ministry would pay my mortgage 15 years later. My sole motivation, since I was a housewife at the time, was to give the Lord my yes to His calling. I submitted to going back to college to become skillful and equipped in serving individuals and families in the ministry of counseling. I obtained a master's and a doctorate degree in an effort to be well trained for His service.

Even during the divorce process, I helped a couple of people at no cost who were in need but couldn't afford to pay. I also applied the sliding scale, reducing the cost for many others, while trusting the Lord to multiply what comes in and to make up the difference in other ways.

I continue to trust the Lord to become completely debt-free, including having the mortgage paid in full. Adding to my faith, He also instructed me to pay a few hundred dollars extra toward the principal of the mortgage each month, which has already saved thousands of dollars and cut years off of the maturity date. I trust God to manifest the answer to my prayer, despite having lost over $250,000 in alimony to date. In full agreement with the Word of God, I am expecting the thief to have to repay me seven times the amount stolen, in the mighty name of Jesus.

> *You can almost excuse a thief if he steals to feed his own family. But if he's caught, he still has to pay back what he stole sevenfold; his punishment and fine will cost him greatly. Don't be so stupid as to think you can get away with your adultery. It will destroy your life, and you'll pay the price for the rest of your days.* (Proverbs 6:30–32 TPT).

The Lord, out of His loving generosity, has also promised to repay me 100 times, and I fully trust and believe Him.

> *"Listen to my words," Jesus said. "Anyone who leaves his home behind and chooses me over children, parents, family, and possessions, all for the sake of the gospel, it will come back to him a hundred times as much in this lifetime—homes, family, mothers, brothers, sisters, children, possessions—along with persecutions. And in the age to come, he will inherit eternal life."* (Mark 10:29–30 TPT)

The Goodness of God

For all three years of the separation and divorce, the Lord showered down peace, mercy, grace, favor, gifts, and blessings from the north, south, east, and west! As previously mentioned, not all of my needs were met immediately, including my need for brakes and a roof. However, His steadfast love and provision were undeniable. Here is a list of testimonies of the goodness of God that showed up in the middle of the divorce process. The Lord sent divine favor, interventions, gifts, and surprises that graciously blessed me. The purpose of sharing these testimonies of God's provision is to prophesy to you that God will also take care of you in the midst of any crisis you may be facing. God causes goodness and mercy to follow after you all of the days of your life, regardless of the circumstances of the season you are in. (See Psalm 23:6.)

1. My sister Deborah opened a credit card account using an offer she'd received with zero percent interest for 18 months. I had hoped to be divorced long before 18 months had passed. This card had a $16,000 credit limit that supplemented my small income through the first year. The first charge paid off a past due balance that my soon-to-be ex neglected to pay at my daughter's university so she could attend her second year of college. I paid the minimum monthly payments on my sister's credit

card, and we scraped by. Unfortunately, the card was already maxed out by the time I needed brakes for my car. After the divorce was finalized, my sister's credit card was the first bill I paid in full.

2. A friend paid a $1,000 contact lens bill that she just happened to read on my refrigerator during a visit to my home. I had it on my refrigerator to remind myself to speak to the mountain of lack and call that bill "paid in full." These specialized, hybrid contact lenses helped me to see clearly for the first time in my life, as I had had keratoconus for decades, which caused my corneas to form a cone shape. When the light hit my corneas, it distorted and blurred my vision. Being able to see clearly helped me get through the mountain of court paperwork and made my life easier to navigate.
3. When I finally had a few hundred dollars available to get new brake pads and rotors, the Lord directed me to a specific brake shop. I wasn't sure I had heard Him clearly, as I found the shop to be rather expensive. However, I felt led to go there, so I went anyway. When the estimate far exceeded the money I had, I assumed I had misheard the Lord. But as I was leaving, a young mechanic approached me as I sat in my car, saying that he was sorry the shop was not able to help me, but he had left a note for me in

my car. The next day, I watched and videotaped this young man completing a full brake job, including new rotors and pads, in my driveway at a fraction of the cost! Glory to God! I tried to hire him for other car repairs months later, and he never responded. Apparently, this was a one-time provision the Lord had set up to take care of the brakes only. Nevertheless, the Lord provided a complete stranger to do the job.

4. My friend, who had been promoted on her job, made a deal with God that included me. She had left a top sales team and was promoted to manage the lowest-producing team. To keep their sales force motivated, the winning sales team was promised an all-expense paid trip with a plus-one in the Caribbean. Unbeknownst to me, my friend promised God that if He helped her team win, she would take *me* with her on vacation. Well, my friend's team won, and I enjoyed five days in Punta Cana, Dominican Republic, at the Hard Rock Resort. This trip included every meal, every coffee, every snack, plus spa treatments, at zero cost to me. My friend even insisted on paying my $30 luggage fee.
5. My daughter Taylor Ashley was blessed to study abroad in Paris, France, for one semester. I kept reminding her that Father God, whom I had raised

her up to know and trust, would remain faithful in this season of her life. My sister insisted that we visit my daughter in Paris for a week, and she paid for everything. I paid her back after the divorce was finalized the following year. My daughter was so happy to have her mom and aunt in Paris that she moved out of her apartment at college and stayed in our hotel room the entire time.

6. A second friend who lived more than 3,000 miles away mailed "happy packages" to me for my birthday, Mother's Day, Valentine's Day, and Christmas. She did this for two and a half years. In addition to various gifts and beauty products, these packages always came loaded with a few hundred dollars in cash!
7. A third friend remained a steady friend who listened, encouraged, and prayed. She also loaned me money a few times but ultimately forgave a third of the debt after she received an inheritance.
8. The woman who helps me clean offered to continue cleaning my home office bi-weekly at no cost as a courtesy to me when I informed her that I couldn't afford her services due to the divorce. I agreed to allow her to keep cleaning; however, I insisted on at least writing checks that she could hold until I had the money to pay. She finally agreed to the

compromise. I had her cash in a few checks at a time, whenever I had the money. When the divorce was over, I instructed her to deposit all of the rest of the checks, but she insisted on tearing up a few.

9. The benevolence fund at my church paid two $1,500 debts that I had.
10. Even though I was awarded my home in the divorce, I was only given three years to qualify as the sole owner on the mortgage. I needed to raise my credit score to 600 before anyone would even consider refinancing the loan. Because my name was also on the mortgage, my credit score plummeted while my home was in foreclosure for three years. Jehovah Jireh, the Lord my Provider, accomplished this feat in half the time, which was right on time to pull equity out for my daughter's wedding. My income-to-debt ratio qualified me by a slim one- to two-percent margin, and I was able to refinance, remove my ex's name, and cut my mortgage rate in half.
11. I'm sure my mother prayed for me every day.

The Lord's tangible compassion and peace were with me every day, and His faithful eyes saw me all the way through. He longs to generously provide for you too, as He is no respecter of persons. (See Acts 10:34 and Romans 2:11.) I have watched many people struggle to fulfill their own destiny or callings because they were emotionally preoccupied with clinging to an abusive, life-draining spouse. That cost is simply too high. Trust me, the goal of marriage is to be a model of Christ's love for the church. Having said all of that, barring unrepentant adultery and severe emotional, physical, or spiritual abuse, by all means stay, pray, and wait for an "egress" or the Lord's successful way out. "Egress," according to *Strong's Exhaustive Concordance* (*ekbasis*, #G1545), is "from a compound of *ek* and the base of *basis* (meaning to go out); an exit (literally or figuratively) – end, way to escape."[4]

Many carnal behaviors are covered in the marital vows under "for better or for worse," which is why I stayed and prayed for decades. At the end of the day, always follow after the peace of God in your spirit versus what your mind, will, and emotions may advise.

Forgiveness and reconciliation are not synonymous. Reconciliation takes two people working together with God to move forward in the same direction. In other words, one person simply cannot reconcile for a healthy marriage. One spouse putting in all of the work and believing that he or she is in control of the spouse's heart or choices is participating in an exercise of futility. The end result is codependency at best, which is toxic and dysfunctional. Codependency is defined by *Merriam-Webster* as "a psychological condition or a relationship in which a person manifesting low self-esteem and a strong desire for approval has an unhealthy attachment to another often controlling or manipulative person."[5]

> *Can two people walk together without agreeing on the direction?* (Amos 3:3 NLT)

If your unsaved or carnal spouse is dwelling peaceably with you, stay and keep praying and seeking Christ-centered counseling with a professional or highly skilled, compassionate pastor. Unfortunately, not all well-meaning clergy qualify for this delicate job.

Forgiveness and reconciliation are not synonymous.

❧

Standing on God's Promises

I meditated on many scriptures during the three-year divorce season. Here are some of my favorites.

> *The very moment I call to you for a father's help the tide of battle turns and my enemies flee. This one thing I know: God is on my side! I trust in the Lord. And I praise him! I trust in the Word of*

God. And I praise him! What harm could man do to me? With God on my side, I will not be afraid of what comes. My heart overflows with praise to God and for his promises. I will always trust in him. So I'm thanking you with all my heart, with gratitude for all you've done. I will do everything I've promised you, Lord. For you have saved my soul from death and my feet from stumbling so that I can walk before the Lord bathed in his life-giving light. (Psalm 56:9–13 TPT)

The one thing I ask of the L*ORD—the thing I seek most—is to live in the house of the* L*ORD all the days of my life, delighting in the* L*ORD's perfections and meditating in his Temple. For he will conceal me there when troubles come; he will hide me in his sanctuary. He will place me out of reach on a high rock. Then I will hold my head high above my enemies who surround me. At his sanctuary I will offer sacrifices with shouts of joy, singing and praising the* L*ORD with music.* (Psalm 27:4–6 NLT)

I love you, L*ORD; you are my strength. The* L*ORD is my rock, my fortress, and my savior; my God is my rock, in whom I find protection. He is my shield, the power that saves me, and my place of safety. I called on the* L*ORD, who is worthy of praise, and he saved me from my enemies.* (Psalm 18:1–3 NLT)

I waited and waited and waited some more, patiently, knowing God would come through for me. Then, at last, he bent down and listened to my cry. He stooped down to lift me out of danger from the desolate pit I was in, out of the muddy mess I had fallen into. Now he's lifted me up into a firm, secure place and steadied me while I walk along his ascending path. A new song for a new day rises up in me every time I think about how he breaks through for me! Ecstatic praise pours out of my mouth until everyone hears how God has set me free. Many will see his miracles; they'll stand in awe of God and fall in love with him! (Psalm 40:1–3 TPT)

By faith these people overthrew kingdoms, ruled with justice, and received what God had promised them. They shut the mouths of lions, quenched the flames of fire, and escaped death by the edge of the sword. Their weakness was turned to strength. They became strong in battle and put whole armies to flight. (Hebrews 11:33–34 NLT)

For your Maker is your Husband—the Lord of hosts is His name—and the Holy One of Israel is your Redeemer; the God of the whole earth He is called. (Isaiah 54:5 AMPC)

Trust in the LORD and do good. Then you will live safely in the land and prosper. Take delight in the LORD, and he will give you your heart's desires. Commit everything you do to the LORD. Trust him, and he will help you. (Psalm 37:3–5 NLT)

For the LORD your God is going with you! He will fight for you against your enemies, and he will give you victory! (Deuteronomy 20:4 NLT)

No one who trusts in you will ever be disgraced, but disgrace comes to those who try to deceive others. (Psalm 25:3 NLT)

He led me to a place of safety; he rescued me because he delights in me. (Psalm 18:19 NLT)

I will praise the LORD at all times. I will constantly speak his praises. ... I prayed to the LORD, and he answered me. He freed me from all my fears. ... The righteous person faces many troubles, but the LORD comes to the rescue each time. (Psalm 34:1, 4, 19 NLT)

Honor me by trusting in me in your day of trouble. Cry aloud to me, and I will be there to rescue you. (Psalm 50:15 TPT)

Practical Life Application

- Forgive without waiting for an apology. Only one person's heartfelt decision in cooperation with the Holy Spirit suffices. It's simply a choice, not a feeling.
- Remember that forgiveness and reconciliation are not synonymous. I encourage forgiveness as a lifestyle in response to anything and everything that anyone does. It must be included when we pray, just as Jesus taught us in the Lord's Prayer. (See Matthew 6:9–13.)
- Continue praying for your spouse, asking God to give him or her wisdom and understanding to know Christ. (See Ephesians 1:16–18.) It is good to pray that light, truth, and revelation intersect your spouse's path and cause him or her to encounter God in a "Damascus road experience" that awakens him or her to righteousness. (See Acts 9:3–9.)
- Avoid manipulation, control, and/or witchcraft prayers and tactics by respecting healthy boundary lines. Do not attempt to usurp your will over your spouse's free will; even God does not do that. For example, I believe that anointing your spouse's pillow with oil is over the line. The main boundary that even God holds Himself back from is a person's

free will. God is not removing anyone's free will to save one's marriage, nor does He do so to save one from an eternity in hell. To ensure that your mind, flesh, and emotions aren't attempting to usurp authority and control over your spouse, I recommend that you pray for him or her mostly in the Holy Spirit. There is no doubt that the Holy Spirit has the ability to pray perfectly higher, better prayers that are far superior to any human effort.

- If you are the one who violated your marital vows, betraying the Lord and your spouse, I encourage you to run to your heavenly Father and repent. Fall on your knees and pursue His truth, which is the Word of God, so that His sword does not fall on you. I encourage you to accept responsibility for your choices and refuse to project blame. The truth is, no one has the power to force you into infidelity. "Temptation comes from our own desires, which entice us and drag us away. These desires give birth to sinful actions. And when sin is allowed to grow, it gives birth to death" (James 1:14–15 NLT).
- I further encourage you to make amends with your children. Ask them to forgive you for burdening them and unleashing hell on them. Lastly, assuming you have followed through on the two earlier recommendations, I encourage you to ask your

spouse to forgive you. Doing so will benefit you and keep you from having to reap what you have sown. "Woe to you, destroyer, you who have not been destroyed. Woe to you, traitor, you who have not been betrayed. When you have finished your work of destroying, you will be destroyed, and when you have completed your betrayal, you will be betrayed" (Isaiah 33:1 TPT).

Chapter 4

The Mind of Christ

There is no question that life on earth is messy and painful. It is filled with all kinds of struggles, losses, and wars. This is because satan is the god of this world. (See 2 Corinthians 4:4.) However, we can learn how to use the authority given to us by Jesus to rule and reign over the enemy. (See Luke 10:19.) The Lord has also promised to be faithful to us during every trial and test, and He has provided a way of escape that leads to victory.

> *We all experience times of testing, which is normal for every human being. But God will be faithful to you. He will screen and filter the severity, nature, and timing of every test or trial you face so that you can bear it. And each test is an opportunity to trust him more, for along with every trial God has provided for you a way of escape that will bring you out of it victoriously.* (1 Corinthians 10:13 TPT)

The Word of God instructs us to *let* the mind of Christ take up residence inside of our minds. (See Philippians 2:5.) Even the most tranquil mind pales in comparison to the mind of Christ. I am convinced that Jesus's mind contains far more peace, wisdom, and clarity then we could ever muster on our own. Reading, meditating, and believing the Word of God is what causes our minds to transform and align with the mind of Christ. The Lord's wisdom stabilizes us and helps us to overcome all challenges, traumas, and adversity. Therefore, it's in our best interests to think in alignment with the mind of Christ. What we think, believe, and say will affect our peace, joy, and even our blood chemistry.

We are also instructed to *set* our minds on the truths and realities of Heaven as we navigate on earth. There's a vortex set up by the adversary that's always swirling and trying to suck us in. "And set your minds and keep them set on what is above (the higher things), not on the things that are on the earth" (Colossians 3:2 AMPC).

The Lord's command is for us to make space for the mind of Christ to take up residence in our minds, then to set and keep our mind on things above. No one can accomplish this *for* us. In other words, we must stop blaming circumstances and other people for the state of our mind. Nothing and no one hold any power over us, unless we have given it to them. The very thought of something or someone controlling me or my mind is problematic. The only persons who are perfect enough to do so and thereby qualify are Father God, Jesus, and the Holy Spirit. Yet, the Trinity are responsible for giving us a free will. They have chosen to hold Themselves behind the same boundary, so we know They did not give anyone or the adversary the right to overstep our free will. That being said, submitting to those in authority is also commanded by God. However, we are not to blindly follow just anyone. We are only to follow others as they follow Christ. (See 1 Corinthians 11:1.) We are to discern every spirit operating inside of a person, regardless of his or her title, to make sure it is the Holy Spirit, an action that is drastically different than just going along. (See 1 John 4:1–5.)

Accept full responsibility for what's in your mind, and if you do not like what is there, the Lord has provided the way for you to return to soundness of mind. If your blood chemistry is out of balance, you probably need to seek holistic or medical help. In my opinion, medication only masks symptoms versus healing root causes. The pharmaceutical industry wants to keep you as a permanent customer for their financial gain. I am not saying that I am against taking pharmaceuticals; there are times when they are absolutely needed. There is also no condemnation on my part for anyone who is taking prescriptions or over-the-counter medication. Lastly, please consult with your primary care physician before even considering a change in medication. My only point here is that there is no healthier way than taking care of your body and learning how to process life via the mind of Christ to enjoy long-term physical, emotional, mental, and spiritual health. Dr. Peter Glidden states that "the third leading cause of death as published in the journal of The American Medical Association is MD directed treatments. This means you go to a medical doctor and an MD gives you treatment and you die from it."[1]

Perhaps you have heard of post-traumatic stress disorder, or PTSD. Trauma and stress are common; everyone can get snagged in trauma, regardless of its size. I highly recommend seeking the medical help you need if you believe you are suffering from PTSD. I would also like to highlight something known as *post-traumatic growth*.

According to the American Psychological Association, post-traumatic growth looks for positive responses in five areas:

1. Appreciation for life
2. Relationships with others
3. New possibilities in life
4. Personal strength
5. Spiritual change[2]

Knowing our options from God's perspective shields us from the lies and taunts from the enemy. Believing the truth sets us free and safeguards us from deceivers and predators as well as self-deception. "Therefore my people go into captivity [to their enemies] without knowing it and because they have no knowledge [of God]" (Isaiah 5:13a AMPC). The Lord is the only source of pure, untainted wisdom, knowledge, and understanding. Agree with this truth deep within your spirit today and ask Him for these manifestations of His Spirit to rest upon you. "And the Spirit of the LORD will rest on him—the Spirit of wisdom and understanding, the Spirit of counsel and might, the Spirit of knowledge and the fear of the LORD" (Isaiah 11:2 NLT). *Strong's Exhaustive Concordance* defines wisdom (*chokmah*, #H2451) in this verse as "skillful, wisdom, wisely, wit."[3] More specifically, *Brown-Driver-Briggs* lists the descriptions of wisdom as "skill in war...wisdom, in administration... shrewdness...prudence in religious affairs...wisdom, ethical and religious."[4]

Here are more definitions from *Strong's Exhaustive Concordance* to help clarify the manifestations of His Spirit that can rest on you as outlined in Isaiah 11:2:

1. Understanding (*binah*, #H998): "knowledge, meaning, perfectly, understanding, wisdom"[5]
2. Counsel (*etsah*, #H6098): "advice, advisement, counselor, purpose"[6]
3. Might (*geburah*, #H1369): "force, mastery, might, mighty act, power, strength"[7]

4. Knowledge (*daath*, #H1847): "cunning...knowledge...wittingly"[8]
5. And the fear (*yirah*, #H3374): "morally, reverence... dreadful...exceedingly, fear"[9]
6. Of the Lord (*Yhvh*, #H3068): "(the) self-Existent or Eternal; Jehovah"[10]

In today's culture, rebellion against God's standards is promoted as progressive. However, it's very sobering to remember that the Word of God equates rebellion with witchcraft. (See 1 Samuel 15:23.) There is nothing progressive about rebellion or its roots in witchcraft. Both are thousands of years old and require little character or no self-control. The choice is ours to conform to cultural norms or to become transformed into the image of Christ. As for me, I have chosen transformation in Christ.

> *Stop imitating the ideals and opinions of the culture around you, but be inwardly transformed by the Holy Spirit through a total reformation of how you think. This will empower you to discern God's will as you live a beautiful life, satisfying and perfect in his eyes.* (Romans 12:2 TPT)

What we think, believe, and say will affect our peace, joy, and even our blood chemistry.

❧

Although the Holy Bible is the most criticized and debated bestseller of all time, it is the most valuable book to live by. I believe the Bible is God-breathed and inspired by God, even though it was penned by flawed human beings. (See 2 Timothy 3:16.) Yet, we need the Holy Spirit to enlighten our understanding of it, since the Bible cannot be intellectually understood. I find it quite telling that the same people who believe that the Bible is a fairytale written by mere men cling to the words of their favorite philosophers as if those words are infallible and all-powerful. To each his own, but the Holy Bible will forever hold unlimited value in my heart. I don't have enough faith to believe philosophers who arrogantly lean on their own understanding and perceptions of "truth."

It's worth noting that biblical meditation is drastically different than cultic and New Age meditative practices. Biblical meditation is choosing to *fill* our mind with biblical truth from God's perspective. Many cultic, New Age, and Eastern meditation practices encourage their followers to *empty* themselves. My concern is that deceptive, disembodied spirits and evil spirits would love to occupy that space.

Biblical meditation involves becoming transformed by renewing our minds as we prefer God's perspective over our own. (See Romans 12:2.) Christians are invited to exchange negative, self-defeating thoughts for the empowering, peaceful thoughts that are found in the mind of Christ. We cannot separate the holy Trinity (Father God, Jesus, and the Holy Spirit) from the Holy Bible. Therefore, Their words will not contradict the truth found in the Holy Bible. It's true that everyone is brainwashed with something. As for me, I'm washing my brain with the Word of God. How about you?

Many New Age and Eastern religions give their followers a mantra. The only words I am repeating are the words of life, truth, and freedom. (See John 6:68–69.) Jesus said, "My sheep listen to my voice; I know them, and they follow me. I give them eternal life, and they will never perish. No one can snatch them away from me, for my Father has given them to me, and he is more powerful than anyone else. No one can snatch them from the Father's hand. The Father and I are one" (John 10:27-30 NLT)

> *My child, will you treasure my wisdom? Then, and only then, will you acquire it. And only if you accept my advice and hide it within will you succeed. So train your heart to listen when I speak and open your spirit wide to expand your discernment—then pass it on to your sons and daughters. ... For if you keep seeking it like a man would seek for*

> *sterling silver, searching in hidden places for cherished treasure, then you will discover the fear of the Lord and find the true knowledge of God. Wisdom is a gift from a generous God, and every word he speaks is full of revelation and becomes a fountain of understanding within you. For the Lord has a hidden storehouse of wisdom made accessible to his godly lovers. He becomes your personal bodyguard as you follow his ways, protecting and guarding you as you choose what is right.* (Proverbs 2:1–2, 4–8 TPT)
>
> *Understand this, my dear brothers and sisters: You must all be quick to listen, slow to speak, and slow to get angry. Human anger does not produce the righteousness God desires. So get rid of all the filth and evil in your lives, and humbly accept the word God has planted in your hearts, for it has the power to save your souls. But don't just listen to God's word. You must do what it says. Otherwise, you are only fooling yourselves.* (James 1:19–22 NLT)

Commanding Your Soul

Human beings are made up of three parts: spirit, soul, and body. More specifically, we are spirit beings created in the image of the only true and living God. We are spiritual beings living inside of physical bodies, and we have a soul. The soul may be defined as the area containing our mind, will, and emotions, or psyche.

> *Now, may the God of peace and harmony set you apart, making you completely holy. And may your entire being—spirit, soul, and body—be kept completely flawless in the appearing of our Lord Jesus, the Anointed One. The one who calls you by name is trustworthy and will thoroughly complete his work in you.* (1 Thessalonians 5:23–24 TPT)

Our God-given responsibility is to nourish our entire being: spirit, soul, and body. One of the best ways to care for our spirit is to live attuned to the Holy Spirit. We learn more of God's ways by studying the Word of God. Another way to feed our spirit is by cultivating a lifestyle of prayer. Praying is simply communicating with our Creator God. Be sure to remember that communication involves talking *and* listening. I encourage you to stay connected and tuned in to the loving help, wisdom, and comfort that is flowing from God's heart to yours 24/7.

One of the best ways to care for your soul is to practice a lifestyle of forgiveness. Trust me, no one and no wrong suffered is worth carrying the heavy chains of bitterness and resentment. The destructive duo of bitterness and resentment only serves to contaminate your entire being and your life. Most people who are unwilling to forgive believe that the person who hurt them does not deserve to be "let off of the hook." The truth is, forgiveness actually unhooks and liberates you.

> *In every relationship be swift to choose peace over competition, and run swiftly toward holiness, for those who are not holy will not see the Lord. Watch over each other to make sure that no one misses the revelation of God's grace. And make sure no one lives with a root of bitterness sprouting within them which will only cause trouble and poison the hearts of many.* (Hebrews 12:14–15 TPT)

The second deterrent to forgiveness is the myth that forgiveness is synonymous with reconciliation. Although we can always choose to forgive (with or without the other person's request, knowledge, or consent), reconciliation requires two people submitted to God and committed to working together by following the same biblical guidelines. Each person must be diligent to follow the process of becoming mentally, emotionally, physically, and spiritually safe enough to be in the relationship. Therefore, forgiveness only takes one heart connected to God, while reconciliation takes two people growing together in the same direction with God.

Some offenses are so diabolical, painful, and destructive that we will need extra supernatural help to fully accomplish forgiveness. Thankfully, God has all of the supernatural power and strength we need to help us forgive and release the person and burden that comes with holding grudges. He is always near and ready to help. "God, you're such a safe and powerful place to find refuge! You're a proven help in time of trouble—more than enough and always available whenever I need you" (Psalm 46:1 TPT).

Our part is to remain willing to forgive, followed by saying in our heart, "I choose to forgive [insert name] for hurting me." Then we must rely on the Holy Spirit to help us to fully accomplish forgiveness and to fully recover. Praying for the offender's well-being is also helpful, along with practicing gratitude for the good he or she brought to your life. It is hard to hold a grudge against someone while praying for that person. However, I highly recommend praying in the Holy Spirit for that person in an effort to keep our mind and emotions out of the equation.

I recommend repeating these three steps as often as needed for as long as needed. The three vital steps to freedom are choosing to forgive, asking God for supernatural help, and praying for the offender. Do not allow your mind or your mouth to replay the details until you need to do so in a therapeutic process. Even then, it is important to choose a therapist who focuses on biblical truths, positive psychology, and post-traumatic growth. When you realize the traumatic event is repeating itself in your mind, interrupt the replay and insert more repentance, forgiveness, and gratitude. You may also ask the Lord to help you to forget the details.

The last deterrent to forgiveness is believing that forgiveness minimizes a person's wrong. It absolutely does not. Authentic forgiveness acknowledges the full weight and depth of the painful offense in an effort to extend forgiveness that parallels. In other words, massive offenses require deep, massive forgiveness.

The three vital steps to freedom are choosing to forgive, asking God for supernatural help, and praying for the offender.

Caring for Your Mind

Although you cannot control the thoughts that flow into your mind, you can absolutely control how you process them and how long you allow them to stay. I encourage you to become proficient at recognizing negative, toxic thought patterns that are vying for your attention. Create a new habit of replacing negative, toxic thoughts with pleasant, peaceful, joyful, thankful, forgiving, and life-giving thoughts. You may find music helpful in diverting your attention. One of the quickest, most effective ways of focusing your thoughts is to sing. The brain has to release the negative thoughts to listen to the words you are singing, especially if you are focusing on maintaining proper pitch and rhythm. I actually enjoy writing new and encouraging jingles and songs in the middle of discouragement. Why lend your imagination to negativity? It's much more peaceful, life-giving, and fun to lend your imagination to creativity. (More details on the benefits of singing are found in Chapter5, "Just Sing.") Until you are reigning over your thoughts and emotions, you won't be able to reign in your life.

I remember writing a spontaneous, jazzy little jingle as I drove in the car. My mind had been attempting to replay something negative that I was tired of thinking about. To force my mind in a different direction, I sang:

I choose to forgive
I choose to forget
I'm keeping my mind
On God's promises
Instead

Yes, feast on all the treasures of the heavenly realm and fill your thoughts with heavenly realities, and

> *not with the distractions of the natural realm.* (Colossians 3:2 TPT)
>
> *A joyful, cheerful heart brings healing to both body and soul. But the one whose heart is crushed struggles with sickness and depression.* (Proverbs 17:22 TPT)
>
> *Don't be impressed with your own wisdom. Instead, fear the LORD and turn away from evil. Then you will have healing for your body and strength for your bones.* (Proverbs 3:7–8 NLT)

Caring for Your Emotions

Grief is one of the most painful emotions. My understanding is that grief activates the same brain circuits as physical pain does, according to neuroscience. Yet, the grieving process cannot be skipped—it may only be delayed. Grieving a loss is not only necessary when a loved one or a pet dies, but it is also a healthy process for when one loses a job, suffers an injury or sickness, becomes an empty nester, becomes divorced, or realizes he or she is getting older. Therefore, grieving is healthy, normal, and necessary. However, it is wise to add prayer and trust in God to the process to avoid getting stuck. Ask for the oil of joy instead of prolonged mourning. (See Isaiah 61:1–3.) Do not isolate yourself, but rather allow healthy friends and family to comfort you. It is good to communicate the details of what is specifically comforting to you. For example, you may ask them to sit quietly and watch a movie with you. Or you may ask them to just listen and not offer advice. I highly recommend that you seek help from licensed, trained professionals or a compassionate, skillful pastor.

Anger is a normal response to loss and is part of the grieving process. However, learning to manage your anger keeps you from ending up with a forest of raging, destructive, and fiery emotions. Remember to choose your thoughts well when processing anger and grief. Emotions are connected to and are the result of one's thinking. Emotional roller coaster rides are draining and disastrous, so I can't recommend ruminating. Once you master the art of managing and refocusing your thoughts, skillful self-regulation will be your reward.

> *So I say to my soul, "Don't be discouraged. Don't be disturbed. For I know my God will break through for me." Then I'll have plenty of reasons to praise him all over again. Yes, he is my saving grace!* (Psalm 42:11 TPT)

Disrobing Shame

Shame is one of the most savage thieves that siphon peace and joy right out of your heart and life. Carrying shame is like carrying a 200-pound mocking monkey on your back that is constantly screaming and whacking you on the head. Where there are family secrets and hiding, you will find shame. The person living in shame has yet to be healed by God's love and forgiveness. That person has neither allowed God's perfect love to cast out fear nor let His cleansing forgiveness wash away shame's vile stench. Christ is not condemning or shaming those who belong to Him. He has set them free from the power of sin, including the sin of carrying shame, condemnation, and self-condemnation. "So now there is no condemnation for those who belong to Christ Jesus. And because you belong to him, the power of the life-giving Spirit has freed you from the power of sin that leads to death" (Romans 8:1–2 NLT).

It's worth noting that shame is found in the "love chapter": "Love does not traffic in shame and disrespect, nor selfishly seek its own honor. Love is not easily irritated or quick to take offense" (1 Corinthians 13:5 TPT).

The bondage of shame affects people's ability to be consistently loving, merciful, and kind toward themselves and others. Those who carry shame are so consumed with hiding it that they often cloak it in arrogance, pride, or false humility. I pray that every reader who is carrying shame today will lay it down, once and for all, never to pick it up again. I encourage you to make the great exchange of cloaks by allowing the Lord to give you double honor for your former shame. Will you accept the Lord's double honor as your new royal robe? Please say "yes" to God's garment, for it is lovingly coordinated with prosperity and everlasting joy!

> *Instead of shame and dishonor, you will enjoy a double share of honor. You will possess a double portion of prosperity in your land, and everlasting joy will be yours.* (Isaiah 61:7 NLT)

It is good to have emotionally, spiritually safe confidants as accountability partners. When we confess our sins to God, He is faithful and just to forgive us and cleanse us from all unrighteousness. (See 1 John 1:9.) Our loving, faithful God then chooses to forget our sins.

> *Where is another God like you, who pardons the guilt of the remnant, overlooking the sins of his special people? You will not stay angry with your people forever, because you delight in showing unfailing love. Once again you will have compassion on us. You will trample our sins under your feet and throw them into the depths of the ocean! You will show us your faithfulness and unfailing*

> *love as you promised to our ancestors Abraham and Jacob long ago.* (Micah 7:18–20 NLT)

However, the Bible also commands us to confess our sins to one another that we may be *healed*. "Confess and acknowledge how you have offended one another and then pray for one another to be instantly healed, for tremendous power is released through the passionate, heartfelt prayer of a godly believer" (James [Jacob] 5:16 TPT).

Since God chooses to forgive, cleanse, and forget our sins, we ought to forget them as well. The accuser hopes to taunt us over our wrongdoings, but he's just a vicious, jealous liar. He hates that we were created in the image of God and he was not. He hates that we can be forgiven and he cannot. Only human beings were purchased and liberated by the blood of Jesus. We have many opportunities, every day, to turn ourselves in and turn our hearts in repentance to our heavenly Father.

> *But if we are living in the light, as God is in the light, then we have fellowship with each other, and the blood of Jesus, his Son, cleanses us from all sin. If we claim we have no sin,* ***we are only fooling ourselves and not living in the truth.*** *But if we confess our sins to him, he is faithful and just to forgive us our sins and to cleanse us from all wickedness. If we claim we have not sinned, we*

> *are calling God a liar and showing that his word has no place in our hearts.* (1 John 1:7–10 NLT, emphasis added)

On the other hand, angels have the *ability* to choose, yet they do not have the *right* to choose. They were created as servants, while we were created as God's children in His likeness and choose to serve Him. Angels were not made in God's image; therefore, there is no forgiveness or second chance for them. This is why, when the archangel lucifer decided that he wanted God's worship, the Bible says that Jesus saw him fall to the ground like lightning. That was it; there was no do-over for him or for the angels that fell with him. (See Luke 10:18–20.)

Any attempt to pay for our own sins by holding ourselves emotionally hostage in shame implies that the blood of Jesus was insufficient. The truth is that in no way could we pay for our sin; attempting to do so is only prideful self-loathing. "We are all infected and impure with sin. When we display our righteous deeds, they are nothing but filthy rags. Like autumn leaves, we wither and fall, and our sins sweep us away like the wind" (Isaiah 64:6 NLT).

Even Jesus had to offload shame in order to carry our sins to the cross. He was crucified, along with the worst criminals and thieves, yet He was completely innocent. He had to focus on the joy of seeing you and me empowered, free, healthy, prospering, and walking in authority in order to accomplish His loving goal. "Looking unto Jesus, the author and finisher of our faith, who for the joy that was set before Him endured the cross, despising the shame, and has sat down at the right hand of the throne of God" (Hebrews 12:2 NKJV). In the aforementioned scripture, the word *despising* is defined by *Strong's Exhaustive Concordance* as "to think against, i.e. Disesteem – despise."[11]

Caring for Your Body

Divine health is God's intention for us. Therefore, He created our body to heal itself. Of course, it needs whole foods, pure water, stress management, and adequate sleep to function at its highest capacity. Whenever sickness, disease, or disorder comes to steal our health, the Lord's wisdom and healing power is accessible to restore us back to wholeness.

Although we've heard this many times, it bears repeating that our bodies also require physical exercise. Rarely do I *feel* like exercising, yet I choose to do so most days as the results are undeniable. We can all find 20 minutes every day for high intensity, interval training (HIIT) (or 40 minutes for a walk). HIIT is "a form of interval training that alternates very brief periods (such as 20 to 40 seconds) of intense exercise at maximum effort with periods (such as 15 to 30 seconds) of less intense exercise."[12] For my HIIT workout, I use a rebounder/mini trampoline to get my heart rate up for 30 seconds. During the 90-second recovery period, I lift 8- to 12-pound weights while marching in place. I also do assisted push-ups leaning against my kitchen counter. Thankfully, we can build muscle at any age.

Taking care of our bodies is also a commandment. "Don't you realize that your body is the temple of the Holy Spirit, who lives in you and was given to you by God? You do not belong to yourself" (1 Corinthians 6:19 NLT).

Love and Acceptance

All human beings need to feel loved, valued, and accepted by others and by God. The Lord lavishes His perfect, pure love on us. I see His love as a continuous deluge of mercy being poured out every moment of every day. To get a glimpse of His overwhelming, unconditional love, picture the water of Niagara Falls as golden honey-oil that is pouring from the throne of God. Through God-illuminated eyes, see His generous outpouring in the width and depth of Niagara Falls, yet multiplied by zillions. See His love, grace, and mercy melting right into the core of your being.

Unfortunately, human beings allow their spiritual perception to become dull, clouded, and even blinded. We allow ourselves to become mentally and emotionally preoccupied with all kinds of noise and nonsense. We give ourselves permission to tune in and out of His ever-flowing love, wisdom, lovingkindness, peace, and joy. By default, we end up settling for only a few splashes of His amazing outpouring. Imagine the benefits we will receive when we position ourselves right under the center of the deluge of God's honey-oil.

Everyone suffers emotional pain. Whether that pain stems from harsh criticism, teasing, humiliation, or rejection from siblings and peers or whether it comes as the result of abuse, neglect, or abandonment from parents, it all wreaks havoc on our self-worth, especially during our formative years. A negative self-image left unchallenged and unhealed programs our inner dialogue to recycle toxic thinking. All of that then festers and deteriorates into a false identity, which works in tandem to undermine our destiny. However, as children of God, we are invited to take part in and experience His divine nature. If you are waiting to attain this nature in Heaven, I recommend looking for opportunities in everyday life to experience His divine nature on earth. As we ask the Holy Spirit to repeatedly fill us with Himself, we become possessed by His loving nature, character, wisdom, and supernatural power. When we are full of Him, we have something of great value to be poured out into our sphere of influence. This result is exactly what our relationship with the Lord was intended to accomplish. We can experience as much or as little of His divine nature as we choose. Let's become spiritual gluttons for His glory! Doing so will increase our capacity to bring the manifestations of Heaven's goodness in supernatural power into the earth realm.

When we are properly yoked with Jesus, He carries the bulk of the weight, which makes His yoke light and easy. Walking right beside Him and enveloped in His glorious presence, life is lighter and easier. We begin to feel the weight of trouble or pain when we attempt to walk in a different direction than He's walking in. We may feel heaviness, pain, and fear when we allow thoughts to remain in our mind that aren't in the mind of Christ. There are no burdensome, fearful thoughts in His mind. I've heard many people describe the journey of faith in Christ as hard. For example, I've heard, "It's hard being a Christian" or "It's so hard to forgive them." Honestly, I find life overwhelmingly easier to navigate when I am walking in the Spirit and in alignment with Christ, compared to the times I have yielded to the dictates of my flesh or emotions. Christ-led steps trump ego-driven steps all day, every day.

Walking in sync with Christ infuses us with peace and strength for the journey. Murmuring, complaining, blame-shifting, and holding grudges create hard, heavy, emotional prisons. They drain all of the peace and joy out of living.

Are you weary, carrying a heavy burden? Come to me. I will refresh your life, for I am your oasis.

Simply join your life with mine. Learn my ways and you'll discover that I'm gentle, humble, easy to please. You will find refreshment and rest in me. For all that I require of you will be pleasant and easy to bear. (Matthew 11:28–30 TPT)

By his divine power, God has given us everything we need for living a godly life. We have received all of this by coming to know him, the one who called us to himself by means of his marvelous glory and excellence. And because of his glory and excellence, he has given us great and precious promises. These are the promises that enable you to ***share his divine nature*** *and escape the world's corruption caused by human desires.* (2 Peter 1:3–4 NLT, emphasis added)

Everything we could ever need for life and godliness has already been deposited in us by his divine power. For all this was lavished upon us through the rich experience of knowing him who has called us by name and invited us to come to him through a glorious manifestation of his goodness. As a result of this, he has given you magnificent promises that are beyond all price, so that through the power of these tremendous promises we can experience partnership with the divine nature, by which you have escaped the corrupt desires that are of the world. (2 Peter 1:3–4 TPT)

Walking in sync with Christ infuses us with peace and strength for the journey.

Misaligned and Maladjusted

Have you allowed your history, circumstances, or emotional wounds to define who you are? If so, I encourage you to challenge and discard every lie that implies you are worthless and insignificant. I assure you, no one was created more valuable than you in the heart of God. His view and truth supersede the opinions of all others, including your own. Accept this truth, believe it, and allow yourself to return to divine wholeness! Even better, please allow yourself to begin thinking, believing, speaking, and behaving like a partner who is sharing in His divine nature.

Perhaps you have allowed poor choices to define you. However, you are not the sum of your negative choices. Great people make atrocious choices sometimes. Many biblical characters have chosen poorly, yet they returned to the

Lord, repented, recovered, and carried on with their assignment. This includes King David, Paul, Peter, King Solomon, and Abraham and Sarah, just to name a few. If you have accepted Jesus as God's Son, then your mistakes have been paid in full, blotted out, and forgotten by God. "I—yes, I alone—will blot out, your sins for my own sake and will never think of them again" (Isaiah 43:25 NLT). "And I will forgive their wickedness, and I will never again remember their sins" (Hebrews 8:12 NLT).

This forgiveness includes the negative choices and mistakes you and I will make in the future. We are all in need of Christ's salvation. Therefore, I highly recommend becoming an excellent receiver of God's generosity, grace, and forgiveness on a continual basis. Why wait another moment?

> *YAHWEH, you are my soul's celebration. How could I ever forget the miracles of kindness you've done for me? You kissed my heart with forgiveness, in spite of all I've done. You've healed me inside and out from every disease. You've rescued me from hell and saved my life. You've crowned me with love and mercy. You satisfy my every desire with good things. You've supercharged my life so that I soar again like a flying eagle in the sky! You're a God who makes things right, giving justice to the defenseless. … Lord, you're so kind and tenderhearted and so patient with people who fail you! Your love is like a*

> *flooding river overflowing its banks with kindness. You don't look at us only to find our faults, just so that you can hold a grudge against us. ... Higher than the highest heavens—that's how high your tender mercy extends! Greater than the grandeur of Heaven above is the greatness of your loyal love, towering over all who fear you and bow down before you! Farther than from a sunrise to a sunset—that's how far you've removed our guilt from us. The same way a loving father feels toward his children—that's but a sample of your tender feelings toward us, your beloved children, who live in awe of you. You know all about us, inside and out. You are mindful that we're made from dust* (Psalm 103:2–6, 8–9, 11–14 TPT)

In addition to repenting and accepting the Lord's forgiveness, forgive yourself and every person of every wrong on a daily basis. As you continue moving forward, I further recommend refraining from sabotaging yourself with poor decisions. Understanding the characteristics and thoughts that sabotage you and the way the enemy works through them is helpful.

Today, I pray that you choose to begin making wise, life-giving choices for yourself, your children, and everyone around you. We are commanded to love God with all of our hearts, souls, minds, and strength, along with loving ourselves and others.

> *"Teacher, which is the most important commandment in the law of Moses?" Jesus replied, "'You must love the* Lord *your God with all your heart, all your soul, and all your mind.' This is the first and greatest commandment. A second is equally important: 'Love your neighbor as yourself.'"* (Matthew 22:36–39 NLT)

Practical Life Application

- Pray, repent, and forgive as a lifestyle.
- Add gratitude to your forgiveness process. Find 3-12 things you are grateful for that are specific to the person you are forgiving.
- Make sure your thoughts are producing peace and not fear.
- Don't believe every thought that comes to your mind. Instead, challenge it and make it align with the truth of God's Word.
- Practice loving yourself, family, friends, and strangers well.

- Manage negative emotions. Don't get sucked into the vortex of anger and fear.
- Pursue healing of all triggers.
- Demonstrate your love for God by obeying Him. (See John 14:15.)
- Make a list of sabotaging thoughts, lies, and fears, and write scriptural truths in response to them.
- Reprogram your inner dialogue to feed you life-giving truth.

Chapter 5

Just Sing

Jesus has shown up for me more times than I can count for all six decades of my life. The consistency of His loving devotion is undeniable. My first desperate need was for enough oxygen just to stay alive. Chronic asthma was the generational curse that ran through my mother's bloodline and manifested in my body within the first few years of my life. The wheezing created by my constricted bronchial tubes was loud, scary, and exhausting. After hours of labored breathing, I desperately needed to escape by falling asleep. At the same time, harassing lies from the enemy yelled that I would die and never awaken again. I distinctly remember saying, many times, "God, I wanna live!"

Asthmatic attacks threatened to smother me to death on a regular basis. Fortunately, Mama's prayers were just as persistent and fervent. She would return home from having worked all day to care for me. She was determined to do anything and everything to help me. The list ran from feeding me—long after I was old enough to feed myself—to slathering my neck, chest, and the roof of my mouth with Mentholatum® under a vapor tent. She made vapor tents with bedsheets and a large pot of boiled water as part of my health care ritual. Mama held me under the vapor tent while praying and rocking me until I fell into a deep sleep. I'm convinced that Mama's prayers preserved me from death by asthmatic attack and by accidental poisoning from Mentholatum®, since the product is actually toxic and should not be ingested. To this day, I cannot stand the smell of mentholated anything, especially petroleum jelly. However, I am very grateful for Mama's prayers and endless efforts to care for me.

God's Comforting Voice

I remember hearing the voice of wisdom guiding me time and again. The Lord often used a simple reference from a cartoon I'd watched of an angel on one shoulder and a devil on the other. The Lord's quiet, soothing voice instructed me to focus on the angel until I fell asleep.

I am forever grateful to have known the Lord as my very present help whenever I had a need. (See Psalm 46:1.) So much of my childhood memories are suppressed from before the age of eight. Life in survival mode caused me to zone out for weeks at a time. There were long stretches of time in bed, measuring every thought and body movement, in order to conserve oxygen. Therefore, I mostly remember bigger, more joyful moments like birthdays, holidays, and being on The Bozo Show. I was healed at age 12 while in the hospital under an oxygen tent for five days. I prayed my very first deeply fervent prayer, and God heard and answered, and I was never imprisoned by asthma again. I have never had another asthmatic attack.

> *God is our Refuge and Strength [mighty and impenetrable to temptation], a very present and well-proved help in trouble.* (Psalm 46:1 AMPC)

These days, worshiping God and making melodies in my heart to Him is particularly special to me because the ability to do so was directly impacted by my healing. With plenty of breath in my lungs, I am forever grateful to be able to sing to my Father God who is holy, beautiful, faithful, and majestic. I will continue giving Him my heartfelt gratitude in worshipful songs, for He has done countless things for me. All of my worship and most of my melodies are for Him and for His glory and honor. He is the One who filled my lungs with His very breath and healed me from chronic asthma. The Lord is worthy regardless, but it's extraordinarily clear to me that He preserved my life and breath to worship Him and to provide encouraging counseling for others.

One of my favorite ways to meditate on the Word of God is by creating jingles and encouraging songs using scriptures. An added benefit to singing Bible verses is that it shuts down worry. It is nearly impossible to worry while singing because your brain has to stop and listen to the melodies coming out of your mouth. The impossibility increases when you are singing on pitch, following a sequence of lyrics and maintaining rhythm.

> *Make the most of every opportunity in these evil days. Don't act thoughtlessly, but understand what the Lord wants you to do. Don't be drunk with wine, because that will ruin your life. Instead, be filled with the Holy Spirit, singing psalms and hymns and spiritual songs among yourselves, and making music to the Lord in your hearts. And give thanks for everything to God the Father in the name of our Lord Jesus Christ.* (Ephesians 5:16–20 NLT)

It is nearly impossible to worry while singing because your brain has to stop and listen to the melodies coming out of your mouth.

In addition to the many spiritual blessings connected to worshiping our Creator, there are many health benefits to singing. Singing causes our brain to release medicine into our brain and blood chemistry.

A study by Harvard Medical School found that singing is a dual hemispheric activity.[1] Apparently, when we sing, our left and right sides of the brain are very busy, which makes it neurologically impossible to have another thought. Sanjay Gupta is a neurosurgeon who studied what music does in the brain specifically and singing in particular. He says:

> If you are speaking, just speaking the words to a song...[it is from] the left temporal lobe, typically in most people. If you're also adding a tune to it, so actually adding the tune of the music to it, that's typically coming from the right parietal lobe. And it's interesting because now you're crossing the midline of the brain. And there aren't a lot of activities where you actually cross the midline of the brain. If you also add a beat to it, some sort of rhythm, that's typically the cerebellum. So here you have a situation now where just by singing a song—and some studies have said just by thinking about singing a song—you can activate so many different areas of the brain. So it's super healthy. It's super good for your brain to sing, sing out loud, put a little rhythm to

> it. It's good for your physical health, but I think even more so for your mental health.[2]

Imagine how exponentially healthy our brain is when we are singing scriptures or worshiping the Lord with a new heart-song. Surely worshiping the King of glory is up on another level, healing our entire spirit, soul, and body.

> *I will exalt you, my God and King, and praise your name forever and ever. I will praise you every day; yes, I will praise you forever. Great is the LORD! He is most worthy of praise! No one can measure his greatness. Let each generation tell its children of your mighty acts; let them proclaim your power. I will meditate on your majestic, glorious splendor and your wonderful miracles. Your awe-inspiring deeds will be on every tongue; I will proclaim your greatness. Everyone will share the story of your wonderful goodness; they will sing with joy about your righteousness. The LORD is merciful and compassionate, slow to get angry and filled with unfailing love. The LORD is good to everyone. He showers compassion on all his creation. All of your works will thank you, LORD, and your faithful followers will praise you. ... For your kingdom is an everlasting kingdom. You rule throughout all generations. The LORD always keeps his promises; he is*

gracious in all he does. ... The L*ORD is righteous in everything he does; he is filled with kindness. The* L*ORD is close to all who call on him, yes, to all who call on him in truth. ... I will praise the* L*ORD, and may everyone on earth bless his holy name forever and ever.* (Psalm 145:1–10, 13, 17–18, 21 NLT)

He said, "You have been given a teachable heart to perceive the secret, hidden mysteries of God's kingdom realm. But to those without a listening heart, my words are merely stories. Even though they have eyes, they are blind to the true meaning of what I say, and even though they listen, they won't receive full revelation." (Luke 8:10 TPT)

Imagine how exponentially healthy and restorative our brain is when we are worshiping the Lord with a new heart-song.

❧

Practical Life Application

- Jingle your way through every day. Sing prayers in your native language and in your Holy Spirit language.
- Remember that singing is great for your mind, emotions, heart, and immune system.
- Practice asking the Lord what He is singing over you.
- Picture His love-songs infusing you with healing oil, freedom, and peace. (See Zephaniah 3:17.)
- Use your vocal cords to make the Lord's songs audible.
- Manage stressors through self-regulation, which includes commanding your mind and emotions to be still and trust God. (See Psalm 46:10.)

For the Lord your God is living among you. He is a mighty savior. He will take delight in you with gladness. With his love, he will calm all your fears. He will rejoice over you with joyful songs. (Zephaniah 3:17 NLT)

"Life is a song, sing it. Life is a struggle, accept it."

—Mother Teresa

Chapter 6

Jesus Is Emotionally Safe

There's no such thing as a spiritually safe Christian who is not *also* emotionally safe. Sadly, who hasn't experienced an unpleasant mixture of poor attitudes and behaviors from believers, including leaders? However, Jesus is spiritually and emotionally safe, and we are called to imitate Him. (See Ephesians 5:1–2.)

People who are emotionally safe are warm, encouraging, and easy to be around. You will know them as you experience God's love flowing through them to you. (See John 13:35.) They value you and honor you as a priceless human being made in the image of their heavenly Father. Emotionally safe people yield to patience and manage their emotions by prioritizing their connection and relationship with you. They are equally as eager to apologize, whether they intended to hurt your feelings or not. They remain loving and agreeable, even when they disagree with you. With emotionally safe people, you won't have to strain to prove to yourself that they value you; rather, their love is consistently accessible, tangible, and in 3-D.

Spiritually safe people are mature, stable, and full of integrity. They have fully surrendered to the Lordship of Jesus, and He is their boss. Although they aren't perfect, they are diligent about their character development and are full of the fruit of the Spirit. Their fruit shows up tangibly in their words, attitudes, and actions. (See Galatians 5:22–23.) Carnal Christians have no shot at emotional or spiritual safety. Carnality and maturity are both choices.

Vine's Expository Dictionary of New Testament Words defines carnal as "governed by human nature, instead of by the Spirit of God."[1]

The fruit or manifestations of an unhealed soul include unmanaged emotions that range from self-pity, anger, bitterness, resentment, oppression, and depression to full-blown rage. Such people tend to be emotionally guarded or detached and struggle to even help themselves. Perhaps this is why the Word of God encourages us to not befriend an angry person. (See Proverbs 22:24.)

The truth is that everyone has an equal opportunity to become offended since rudeness is plentiful on the earth. It is impossible to avoid anger, pain, and suffering. However, we can choose forgiveness, healing, transformation, and restoration. Once we are adults, it is 100% our responsibility to learn how to respond to anger, pain, and suffering in healthy ways. Only then can we live unencumbered and whole in Christ. No one can accomplish this righteous living by themselves. We all need help from the Lord, His Word, and those who are called, anointed, and equipped to help facilitate our recovery from all of life's traumas. Just like we are hurt within relationships with people, we are also healed within relationships with emotionally and spiritually safe people.

> *The Holy Spirit of God has sealed you in Jesus Christ until you experience your full salvation. So never grieve the Spirit of God or take for granted his holy influence in your life. Lay aside bitter words, temper tantrums, revenge, profanity, and insults. But instead be kind and affectionate toward one another. Has God graciously forgiven you? Then graciously forgive one another in the depths of Christ's love.* (Ephesians 4:30–32 TPT)

When I was growing up, I was alarmed by the vast number of emotionally unstable and unsafe people there were, even at church. It saddens me that the church at large still has not matured to the point of developing the character of Christ or the fruit of the Spirit to change this imbalance. Unbelievers continue to mock the church for double standards and the ever-unfolding scandals. The Bible says we are blessed when people say all manner of evil about us *falsely* for the sake of the gospel. There is no blessing when their words are true.

> *Blessed (happy, to be envied, and spiritually prosperous—with life-joy and satisfaction in God's favor and salvation, regardless of your outward conditions) are you when people revile you and persecute you and say all kinds of evil things against you* ***falsely*** *on My account.* (Matthew 5:11 AMPC, emphasis added)

My prayer is that every reader will become intentional about maturing into an emotionally and spiritually safe, mature person. This change does not automatically happen when we say the salvation prayer. The only automatic blessing we receive after praying the salvation prayer is obtaining access to eternity in Heaven. To enjoy more of the salvation package on earth requires submission to God and His process of transformation. Surrender is an important step since we draw the boundaries that the Lord is allowed to work within, in our lives. This is clearly seen when Jesus could only heal a few people in His hometown right after healing multitudes of people in other places. When Jesus walked through the city gates of His hometown, people only saw Mary's "illegitimate" son. The gossip surrounding her pregnancy probably continued to swirl in the minds of the people. Surely, the good news of multitudes being healed had reached them, yet they could not spiritually perceive Him as their Healer and definitely not as their Messiah.

> *Jesus left that part of the country and returned with his disciples to Nazareth, his hometown. The next Sabbath he began teaching in the synagogue, and many who heard him were amazed. They asked, "Where did he get all this wisdom and the power to perform such miracles?" Then they scoffed, "He's just a carpenter, the son of Mary and the brother of James, Joseph, Judas, and Simon. And his sisters live right here among us." They were deeply offended and refused to believe in him. Then Jesus told them, "A prophet is honored everywhere except in his own hometown and among his relatives and his own family."* ***And because of their unbelief, he couldn't do any miracles among them*** *except to place his hands on a few sick people and heal them. And he was amazed at their unbelief.* (Mark 6:1–6 NLT, emphasis added)

Become intentional about maturing into an emotionally and spiritually safe, mature person.

❧

Why not intentionally enlarge the space in your heart and mind that you give to the Lord? Why not stretch your capacity far and wide, so His glory may be seen in your life? Unbelief is a powerful hindrance that blocks the very breakthrough you need, a breakthrough that has already been purchased by the blood of Jesus. Unbelief also produces substance in your heart, mind, and life. You do not want to be an unbelieving believer. Instead, choose to continuously be filled by the Spirit of God and live on His altar of holy fire. Those who are half in and half out are lukewarm, which is vomitus to God. "I know all that you do, and I know that you are neither frozen in apathy nor fervent with passion. How I wish you were either one or the other! But because you are neither cold nor hot, but lukewarm, I am about to spit you from my mouth" (Revelation 3:15–16 TPT).

If you have settled for lukewarm, religious activity, today is a great day to change your mind. If you are miserable, poor, busted, and disgusted, Jesus's solution is for you to repent and pursue His kingdom and righteousness. You must purchase heavenly eye salve via a laid-down life that's been purified by holy fire so you can perceive His truth. This is not attainable through carnal Christian living, a drive-through church service, or in a prayer line.

> *For you claim, "I'm rich and getting richer—I don't need a thing." Yet you are clueless that you're miserable, poor, blind, barren, and naked! So I counsel you to purchase gold perfected by fire, so that you can be truly rich. Purchase a white garment to cover and clothe your shameful Adam-nakedness. Purchase eye salve to be placed over your eyes so that you can truly see. All those I dearly love I unmask and train. So repent and be eager to pursue what is right. Behold, I'm standing at the door, knocking. If your heart is open to hear my voice and you open the door within, I will come in to you and feast with you, and you will feast with me.* (Revelation 3:17–20 TPT)

No matter what condition your life is in, Jesus is your hope. Every day we can return to Him and ask for a divine restart. "And you, because of my blood covenant with you, I'll release your prisoners from their hopeless cells. Come home, hope-filled prisoners! This very day I'm declaring a double bonus—everything you lost returned twice-over!" (Zechariah 9:11–12 MSG) Leave behind every sinful passion, attitude, and person who is hindering you from following passionately after Christ. Jesus has promised to restore everything back that was lost, multiplied 100 times!

> *And everyone who has given up houses or brothers or sisters or father or mother or children or property, for my sake, will receive a* ***hundred times as much in return and will inherit eternal life****. But many who are the greatest now will be least important then, and those who seem least important now will be the greatest then.* (Matthew 19:29–30 NLT, emphasis added)

Many Christians only enjoy one part of salvation, which is their ticket to Heaven when they die. However, one of the names of God is Jehovah, which means salvation. Biblical salvation is a package deal. This generous, gracious gift was purchased by the blood of Jesus and was meant to be enjoyed while on earth. Heaven's atmosphere is already super-infused with everything good and is lacking nothing. Salvation means "rescue or safety (physically or morally) – deliver, health, salvation, save, saving."[2] Where there is stealing, killing, and destroying, so is there the work of the adversary. Where there is life, joy, peace, prosperity, and everything good, there the loving hand of God is made known. The blood of Jesus is the doorway right into the throne room of God. Jesus Himself said, "The thief's purpose is to steal and kill and destroy. My purpose is to give them a rich and satisfying life" (John 10:10 NLT). "Whatever is good and perfect is a gift coming down to us from God our Father, who created all the lights in the heavens. He never changes or casts a shifting shadow" (James 1:17 NLT).

No matter what condition your life is in, Jesus is your hope.

❧

Moving Forward Undaunted

Can you imagine being beaten, whipped, and crucified, especially having done nothing wrong? Me neither! However, Jesus did a beautiful job of walking out a sinless life on earth as the Son of man. Sometimes we forget that He laid down His deity and supernatural power and was birthed by a mere woman, just like you and I were. Therefore, He could do *nothing* unless the Lord empowered Him to do it, just like you and me. "So Jesus said, 'I speak to you eternal truth. The Son is unable to do anything from himself or through his own initiative. I only do the works that I see the Father doing, for the Son does the same works as his Father'" (John 5:19 TPT).

Can you imagine being imprisoned, yet still full of peace and joy to the point that you begin to sing? Me neither! However, Paul's spiritual walk encourages me to follow even harder after Christ. His focus, tenacity, and worship so moved the heart of God that God sent a chain-breaking earthquake that opened every prison door. As a result, Paul, Silas, and every other prisoner were delivered from captivity. We too can stay focused and grow in our purpose by trusting God to free not only us, but also everyone around us.

> *Around midnight Paul and Silas were praying and singing hymns to God, and the other prisoners were listening. Suddenly, there was a massive earthquake, and the prison was shaken to its foundations. All the doors immediately flew open, and the chains of every prisoner fell off! The jailer woke up to see the prison doors wide open. He assumed the prisoners had escaped, so he drew his sword to kill himself. But Paul shouted to him, "Stop! Don't kill yourself! We are all here!" The jailer called for lights and ran to the dungeon and fell down trembling before Paul and Silas. Then he brought them out and asked, "Sirs, what must I do to be saved?" They replied, "**Believe in the Lord Jesus and you will be saved, along with everyone in your household.**" ... The next morning the city officials sent the police to tell the jailer, "Let those men*

go!" So the jailer told Paul, "The city officials have said you and Silas are free to leave. Go in peace." But Paul replied, "They have publicly beaten us without a trial and put us in prison—and we are Roman citizens. So now they want us to leave secretly? Certainly not! Let them come themselves to release us!" When the police reported this, the city officials were alarmed to learn that Paul and Silas were Roman citizens. So they came to the jail and apologized to them. Then they brought them out and begged them to leave the city. When Paul and Silas left the prison, they returned to the home of Lydia. There they met with the believers and encouraged them once more. Then they left town. (Acts 16:25–31, 35–40 NLT, emphasis added)

Practical Life Application

- Practice surrendering your will to God's will and way.
- Require yourself to become emotionally and spiritually healthy.
- Allow Jesus to be Lord over your attitude, emotions, and life.
- Refuse to sabotage yourself or others. Be kind.

- Acknowledge that you are never without hope—His name is Jesus. Accept Him.
- Confess and repent to God and allow Him to cleanse you. (See 1 John 1:9.)

Chapter 7

Cultivating Joy

Your level of joy is very important to God. There are more than 400 references to the word *joy* in the Bible, including various forms of the word like *enjoy*, *joyful*, and *rejoice*. Joy is your portion where weariness wants to make itself at home. Joy was meant to be the sustaining strength of your life. Today is a great day to awaken joy in your heart, home, and relationships.

To begin awakening joy, you must understand that when the Holy Spirit came to live inside of you, joy came to live inside of you also. I encourage you to yield to joy right in the middle of frustration. This causes your joy to mature, and your joyful response frustrates the enemy instead of frustrating you! Of course, grieving a loss is healthy, normal, and necessary. Therefore, I am not suggesting that you *pretend* you are not frustrated, sad, or in pain. Instead, I recommend acknowledging, validating, and feeling your feelings. At the same time, I recommend doing so in the presence of the Father, Jesus, and the Holy Spirit.

I also recommend setting a time limit on feeling your feelings. Intentionally give more time and *access* to God than to the adversary, that you may endure suffering. Ask God for the oil of joy instead of enduring a prolonged mourning of a loss; allow the Holy Spirit and others to comfort you. Do not isolate or give space for a deceptive spirit of grief to come in and set up camp in your life. I encourage you to seek help from licensed, trained professionals. Empathetic friends can also be very helpful. I was an empathetic, nurturing, stable friend, full of encouragement and the Word of God, decades before I became a licensed, commissioned, and board-certified counselor by the National Christian Counselors Association. I believe every believer is chosen for this compassionate assignment according to the following scripture:

> *The Spirit of the Lord God is upon me, because the Lord has anointed and qualified me to preach the Gospel of good tidings to the meek, the poor, and afflicted; He has sent me to bind up and heal the brokenhearted, to proclaim liberty to the [physical and spiritual] captives and the opening of the prison and of the eyes to those who are bound, to proclaim the acceptable year of the Lord [the year of His favor] and the day of vengeance of our God, to*

> *comfort all who mourn, to grant [***consolation and joy***] to those who mourn in Zion—to give them an ornament (a garland or diadem) of beauty instead of ashes, the* ***oil of joy*** *instead of mourning, the garment [expressive] of praise instead of a heavy, burdened, and failing spirit—that they may be called oaks of righteousness [lofty, strong, and magnificent, distinguished for uprightness, justice, and right standing with God], the planting of the Lord, that He may be glorified.* (Isaiah 61:1–3 AMPC, emphasis added)

Jesus said that we would do even greater works than He did. (See John 14:12.) Therefore, although the scripture in Isaiah 61 is about Jesus, it fully applies to every believer as well.

Start today to choose to practice yielding to joy. While practicing and cultivating joy, you are creating patterns of thinking or habit structures that occupy physical real estate in your brain. Think about what you have been practicing. Prayerfully, you have not been practicing murmuring, complaining, and worrying! Those simply won't help you. Perhaps read how the Israelites' murmuring, complaining, and blaming God worked for them. (See Numbers 14:26–45.) Bible scholars calculate that God planned an 11-day journey straight through the wilderness and into the

Promised Land. Murmuring and complaining turned an 11-day trip into 40 years of wandering in a vicious cycle! To avoid negative cycles, keep your mind, heart, and eyes on the One who holds solutions to your problems. If your problems look mountainous, change what you're focusing on. Choose to magnify Jesus! (See Psalm 34.)

> *Pour out all your worries and stress upon him and leave them there, for he always tenderly cares for you.* (1 Peter 5:7 TPT)

God Is Joyful

The Most High God is overflowing with joy! He is not oppressed, depressed, fearful, angry, or lethargic. Because the adversary cannot do anything to change the shalom of God, the adversary hopes to frustrate, scare, oppress, depress, disturb, and ultimately destroy those who are closest to God's heart: you and I.

Ask yourself these questions: Is joy alive and well in me? Am I enjoying life and bringing joy into the lives of others? I encourage you to be honest with yourself. You may also want to ask a few healthy, loving, honest friends and family members how they would rank your level of joy. An outside perspective from those you trust may be eye-opening. Although your joy may have leaked out over the years and may have felt out of reach, Father God has enough power and healing balm to restore it as you return to your inheritance of joy in the Lord. Joy releases medicine into your brain and blood chemistry. "A happy heart is good medicine and a cheerful mind works healing, but a broken spirit dries up the bones" (Proverbs 17:22 AMPC).

Whenever your heart and home are in need of joy, begin to think about the goodness of the Lord and usher in His presence with heartfelt prayers and songs of gratitude. One moment in His presence can change the entire trajectory of your life. The Lord wants His children to experience Him, to be enveloped in His presence. Even after one glorious encounter with Him, no one will ever be able to explain Him away. Your heavenly Father surrounds you and fills you with Himself, and He places your feet on the path to life. "You will show me the path of life; in Your presence is fullness of joy; at Your right hand are pleasures forevermore" (Psalm 16:11 NKJV).

Using *Strong's Exhaustive Concordance*, I looked up many of the words in Psalm 16:11 to gain more understanding. Doing this is helpful because words are commonly left out when translating from one language to another. Here are the Hebrew definitions I found:

1. Life (*chay*, #H2416): "alive...fresh...strong...merry... quick...springing"[1]

2. Presence (*panim* or *paneh*, #H6440): "face, favour... forefront"[2]
3. Joy (*simchah*, #H8057): "glee...exceeding(-ly), gladness, joy(-fulness)"[3]
4. Right (*yamin*, #H3225): "the right hand...(as the stronger and more dexterous)"[4]
5. Pleasures (*na'iym*, #H5273): "delightful...pleasant... sweet"[5]
6. Evermore (*netsach*, #H5331): "continually (i.e. To the most distant point of view)...constantly... perpetual, strength, victory"[6]

With the added clarification from these definitions, here is a declaration from Psalm 16:11. I encourage you to declare this over yourself:

> Father God, thank You for showing me the path to fresh, strong, quick, springing merriment, which is found in the forefront of Your face and favor. Your face and favor are full of glee and gladness, which makes me exceedingly joyful! In Your stronger, skillful, artful, and more competent right hand are delightful, pleasant, and sweet blessings that are bringing me constant, perpetual strength and victory all the way to the

> end of my destiny! Thank You, Father, in Jesus's name. Amen!

Even in the midst of evil, God's level of joy is obviously not affected. It's no secret that wicked people plot against God's people. But did you know that the Lord is far from depressed over this fact? Instead, the Lord laughs at the wicked because He sees the adversary's day is coming. "Bad guys have it in for the good guys, obsessed with doing them in. But GOD isn't losing any sleep; to him they're a joke with no punch line" (Psalm 37:13 MSG).

When we talk to God, He answers and shows up with exactly what we need. Whenever our circumstances disagree with this truth, please remember that there are many variables. The first place I look when there is a discrepancy is within myself. If I find an issue, I repent. I refuse to allow my circumstances to tell me who God is. Instead, I take Him at His Word, since the Lord is the only rock-solid source of truth, wisdom, and faithfulness. "Cry out to me and I will answer you. I will reveal to you great things, guarded secrets that you never could have known" (Jeremiah 33:3 TPT). "I was desperate for you to help me in my struggles, and you did!" (Psalm 120:1 TPT) The only way to access God is to walk right through the door that He has provided. Jesus is the doorway to God, and He wants to become your best friend. (See John 10:9.) Therefore, run through the door that the Father has provided. Do not stumble around in darkness, assuming you can figure it out on your own or that some arrogant philosopher, who was created by God, can be your source of truth or wisdom.

The Lord is the only rock-solid source of truth, wisdom, and faithfulness.

❧

Count It All Joy

You may not be able to laugh at the enemy and his evil plans right now. But in the meantime, the Bible encourages us to "count it all joy" when trials come our way (James 1:2 NKJV). We can allow ourselves to return to joy by trusting His process. The Word of God explains the process this way:

1. Pressure, affliction, and hardship produce patience and unswerving endurance.
2. Endurance develops maturity of character, faith, and integrity.
3. Character produces confident hope of eternal salvation.

> *Moreover [let us also* ***be full of joy now!****] let us exult and triumph in our troubles and rejoice in our sufferings, knowing that pressure and affliction and hardship produce patient and unswerving endurance. And endurance (fortitude) develops maturity of character (approved faith and tried integrity). And character [of this sort] produces [the habit of] joyful and confident hope of eternal salvation. Such hope never disappoints or deludes or shames us, for God's love has been poured out in our hearts through the Holy Spirit Who has been given to us.* (Romans 5:3–5 AMPC, emphasis added)
>
> *My fellow believers, when it seems as though you are facing nothing but difficulties, see it as an invaluable opportunity to experience the greatest joy that you can! For you know that when your faith is tested it stirs up in you the power of endurance. And then as your endurance grows even stronger, it will release perfection into every part of your being until there is nothing missing and nothing lacking.* (James [Jacob] 1:2–4 TPT)

The adversary will use every evil, deceptive tactic he knows in an effort to plunder, kill, and destroy you. He will never show you mercy; therefore, you must never show him mercy. Don't give him access by believing and agreeing with his lies. Fortunately, we have been given an unfair advantage over him, which was purchased by the blood of Jesus.

> *Be well balanced and always alert, because your enemy, the devil, roams around incessantly, like a roaring lion looking for its prey to devour. Take a decisive stand against him and resist his every attack with strong, vigorous faith. For you know that your believing brothers and sisters around the world are experiencing the same kinds of troubles you endure. And then, after your brief suffering, the God of all loving grace, who has called you to share in his eternal glory in Christ, will personally and powerfully restore you and make you stronger than ever. Yes, he will set you firmly in place and build you up.* (1 Peter 5:8–10 TPT)

Has the enemy stolen your joy? If so, start declaring out loud that your joy will be restored seven times. "But if he is found out, he must restore seven times [what he stole]; he must give the whole substance of his house [if necessary—to meet his fine]" (Proverbs 6:31 AMPC). According to this scripture, when your joy is restored, it opens the floodgates for full restoration of everything that was stolen.

Joy was meant to be the sustaining strength of your life.

If your joy has been stolen, see the adversary as the thief. The enemy often works through people, but they are just marionettes along for the ride. Forgive the people, set healthy boundaries with them, and use your authority over the adversary, demanding that he repay.

> *A thief has only one thing in mind—he wants to steal, slaughter, and destroy. But I have come to give you everything in abundance, more than you expect—life in its fullness until you overflow! I am the Good Shepherd who lays down my life as a sacrifice for the sheep.* (John 10:10–11 TPT)
>
> *...And be not grieved and depressed, for the joy of the Lord is your strength and stronghold.* (Nehemiah 8:10 AMPC)

When the Holy Spirit comes to live in your heart, He brings His fruit with Him. We have an unlimited passport provided by the blood of Jesus. We can run through the door (Jesus) and into the Lord's enriching presence to receive everything we need, including joy.

> *But the fruit produced by the Holy Spirit within you is divine love in all its varied expressions:* ***joy that overflows****, peace that subdues, patience that endures, kindness in action, a life full of virtue, faith that prevails, gentleness of heart, and strength of spirit. Never set the law above these qualities, for they are meant to be* ***limitless****.* (Galatians 5:22–23 TPT, emphasis added)

Do you know how the fruit of the Spirit grows and matures to the point when we may enjoy it? I believe as we practice yielding to the Holy Spirit, right in the middle of the circumstance, the fruit of the Spirit matures and becomes more readily available for you and others to enjoy! God wants *you* to be the first one to be blessed by a bumper crop of joy! Let me ask you another question: Whom does God command us to love our neighbors as? (See Mark 12:30–31.) Most people know that we are to love our neighbor as *ourselves*. I am convinced that God was *not* confused about the order.

Some of you will need to simply allow yourselves to return to joy. You will need to give yourself permission to rejoice again after having endured a major loss or suffered a trauma or tragedy.

As I mentioned at the beginning of this chapter, grieving a loss is healthy, normal, and necessary. Trying to bypass the grieving process only suppresses and delays it. Rather than have unprocessed grief resurface down the road in a more costly and destructive way, it's better to acknowledge and feel your emotions than to suppress them. However, I highly recommend adding prayer and faith to the process of grieving to avoid getting stuck. It's good to remember that the length of time you grieve the loss of a loved one does not reflect the depth of your love. Giving yourself permission to grieve in a healthy manner and expecting yourself to fully recover is exactly what your loved one wants for you. Even the most devout Christians seem to forget that Jesus bore our griefs and sorrows on the cross as much as He carried our sins. I fully believe that He did the bulk of the heavy lifting to keep the weight of grief from completely devastating and crushing us. "Surely He has borne our griefs and carried our sorrows; yet we esteemed Him stricken, smitten by God, and afflicted" (Isaiah 53:4 NKJV).

The enemy automatically assumes that your grieving season is his open season to torture you. Don't grant the enemy access to you in *any* season. Give him no space or place, ever. (See Ephesians 4:27.) When you are grieving, expect the Comforter, the Holy Spirit, to draw even closer to you to provide supernatural comfort. Ask the Lord for the oil of joy instead of prolonged mourning of losses. (See Isaiah 61:1–3.) Please do not isolate yourself; rather, allow healthy friends and family to comfort you. It is good to specifically communicate what is comforting to you. For example, you may ask them to just sit quietly with you and watch a movie. Or you may ask them to simply listen and not offer advice. You may ask them to just hold you while you cry. The Lord wants you blessed and comforted when you mourn. "God blesses those who mourn, for they will be comforted" (Matthew 5:4 NLT). I have mentioned this before, but it bears repeating.

Anger is a normal response to loss and is part of the grieving cycle. However, learning to manage your anger will keep you from being held captive by it. Feeling anger is not a sin. Staying angry and allowing that anger to control you, however, is a sin. Allowing the enemy to put you in a stronghold for any reason is costly. "And 'don't sin by letting anger control you.' Don't let the sun go down while you are still angry, for anger gives a foothold to the devil" (Ephesians 4:26–27 NLT).

I also highly recommend seeing a licensed, trained professional or an empathetic, skilled friend or pastor for help. "So don't go to war without wise guidance; victory depends on having many advisers" (Proverbs 24:6 NLT). "Listen well to wise counsel and be willing to learn from correction so that by the end of your life you'll be known for your wisdom" (Proverbs 19:20 TPT).

I'm also not suggesting that you rush through the grieving process. I am encouraging you to choose and to expect to fully recover. Instead of allowing yourself to get stuck in the grieving process, may I recommend hosting a celebratory memorial or making a donation to a charity in honor of your loved one? The memory of your loved one will be greatly honored, and you may then focus on fully living again. Do not lend your imagination to reviewing the saddest memories. Instead, use your imagination to enjoy happier memories with your loved one and to dream about all of the splendor your loved one is enjoying in Heaven.

Prayerfully, you will allow yourself to cycle through the process of grief. Decide that you will cycle out of mourning and into joy. Ask the Holy Spirit to help you. He is the most awesome Comforter.

> *But the Comforter (Counselor, Helper, Intercessor, Advocate, Strengthener, Standby), the Holy Spirit, Whom the Father will send in My name [in My place, to represent Me and act on My behalf], He will teach you all things. And He will cause you to recall (will remind you of, bring to your remembrance) everything I have told you.* (John 14:26 AMPC)

Resetting Your Focus

It is true that the enemy is allowed to send negative, fearful, and sad thoughts to your mind. Yet not all negative, fearful, and sad thoughts are from the enemy. Unresolved grief, bitterness, and toxic mindsets also serve up the same garbage. It is also true that you alone choose how you process thoughts and decide how long those thoughts stay. The adversary has zero power and zero authority to keep his lies going in *your* mind. He needs your attention and agreement because he cannot violate your God-given free will. When you choose to focus on an offense, loss, or painful circumstance, you will have emotions and feelings that match. It's simply the way your brain is wired. Instead, choose to renew your mind with God's truth or by refocusing on anything that is good, lovely, funny, or uplifting. (See Philippians 4:6–9.) I encourage you to choose life and life-giving thoughts today and every day.

> *Don't be pulled in different directions or worried about a thing. Be saturated in prayer throughout each day, offering your faith-filled requests before God with overflowing gratitude. Tell him every detail of your life, then God's wonderful peace that transcends human understanding, will guard your heart and mind through Jesus Christ. Keep your thoughts continually fixed on all that is authentic and real, honorable and admirable, beautiful and respectful, pure and holy, merciful and kind. And fasten your thoughts on every glorious work of God, praising him always. Put into practice the example of all that you have heard from me or seen*

> *in my life and the God of peace will be with you in all things.* (Philippians 4:6–9 TPT)

Awaken every day and choose life and peace.

> *Today I have given you the choice between life and death, between blessings and curses. Now I call on Heaven and earth to witness the choice you make. Oh, that you would choose life, so that you and your descendants might live! You can make this choice by loving the Lord your God, obeying him, and committing yourself firmly to him. This is the key to your life. And if you love and obey the* Lord, *you will live long in the land the* Lord *swore to give your ancestors Abraham, Isaac, and Jacob.* (Deuteronomy 30:19–20 NLT)

I firmly believe that healing was purchased on the cross for everyone. The blood of Jesus purchased healing for your mind, emotions, and body. The root word for salvation is the Greek word *sózó*, which means "to save, to keep safe and sound, to rescue from danger or destruction…to save a suffering one (from perishing), e.g. one suffering from disease, to make well, heal, restore to health…to preserve one who is in danger of destruction, to save (i.e. rescue)."[7]

Prayerfully, this more detailed definition of salvation helps you understand and believe that Jesus purchased much more than your ticket to Heaven. Jesus Himself taught us to pray, "Thy kingdom come, Thy will be done *in earth, as it is in Heaven*" (Matthew 6:10 KJV, emphasis added). Surely, we can all agree that there is no sickness in Heaven. Therefore, we may pray that our entire being and earth realm line up with Heaven's reality. By the stripes on Jesus's back, we are healed. "But he was pierced for our rebellion, crushed for our sins. He was beaten so we could be whole. He was whipped so we could be healed" (Isaiah 53:5 NLT).

Is All This Joy Really God's Idea?

Not only is overflowing joy a God-idea, it's actually what the King's domain *is*. "For the Kingdom of God is not a matter of what we eat or drink, but of living a life of goodness and peace and joy in the Holy Spirit" (Romans 14:17 NLT).

When life gets tough, I encourage you to keep track of how quickly you return to peace and joy. Resisting the enemy at his onset is much easier than waiting an hour, day, week, month, or year. However, you will not be able to fully resist him if you have not first submitted to God. "So humble yourselves before God. Resist the devil, and he will flee from you" (James 4:7 NLT). You can't collaborate with the enemy one minute and resist him the next. He will laugh at you and continue harassing you.

Why wait until you have a stronghold (a fortified castle of fear and lies) surrounding you? Make it your goal to shorten the trip back to joy. My personal goal is to do so in less than 15 minutes. Do not stew until your friend has time to show up with an encouraging word or until you get to church or therapy. Use your blood-bought authority right away! You might as well run straight to Jesus yourself as He alone has the words of life. "Simon Peter replied, 'Lord, to whom would we go? You have the words that give eternal life. We believe, and we know you are the Holy One of God'" (John 6:68–69 NLT).

You can't collaborate with the enemy one minute and resist him the next. He will laugh at you and continue harassing you.

❧

At times, King David was up, then down, and then emotionally all over the place. There were times when he was not emotionally or spiritually safe, not even for himself. However, he created a lifestyle of running to the Lord for forgiveness and help. He also created the habit of encouraging and strengthening himself in the Lord. "Now David was greatly distressed, for the people spoke of stoning him, because the soul of all the people was grieved, every man for his sons and his daughters. But David strengthened himself in the Lord his God" (1 Samuel 30:6 NKJV). God called David a man after His own heart, not an emotional mess. "But now your kingdom must end, for the Lord has sought out a man after his own heart. The Lord has already appointed him to be the leader of his people, because you have not kept the Lord's command" (1 Samuel 13:14 NLT).

Healthy Interdependence

The Lord created us to live connected in community with healthy interdependent relationships. In healthy relationships, there is a mutual interdependence, respect, and honor with complete dependence on God alone. Medical science has provided helpful research as well. One source states that social connections help "relieve harmful levels of stress, which can adversely affect coronary arteries, gut function, insulin regulation, and the immune system."[8] "And become useful and helpful and kind to one another, tenderhearted (compassionate, understanding, loving-hearted), forgiving one another [readily and freely], as God in Christ forgave you" (Ephesians 4:32 AMPC).

> *For this reason the Lord is still waiting to show his favor to you so he can show you his marvelous love. He waits to be gracious to you. He sits on his throne ready to show mercy to you. For Yahweh*

> *is the Lord of justice, faithful to keep his promises. Overwhelmed with bliss are all who will entwine their hearts in him, waiting for him to help them.* (Isaiah 30:18 TPT)

Many years ago, I heard the Lord say, "*Many of My loved ones are caught up in drama, when I intended for them to enjoy musicals instead.*" I understood that to mean that the Lord wants us to respond in life, even in times of trouble, with heartfelt worship to Him. Imagine the shock the enemy receives when we learn to respond to his lies, accusations, and drama with praises to the Lord. Wherever the Lord has dominion is His kingdom, and that includes the mental space we give Him in our minds. The kingdom of God is righteousness, peace, and *joy in* the Holy Spirit. (See Romans 14:17.)

One of the enemy's favorite things to bait us with is worry, which is fear. Not only is worrying evidence of unbelief, but it is also a form of worship. Whatever holds the majority of our attention becomes idolatrous. Lastly, worry poisons our immune system with toxins, which can affect every system in our bodies. Perhaps this is why Jesus tells us in His own words not to worry about the things that consume the minds of unbelievers.

> *That is why I tell you not to worry about everyday life—whether you have enough food and drink, or*

> *enough clothes to wear. Isn't life more than food, and your body more than clothing? Look at the birds. They don't plant or harvest or store food in barns, for your heavenly Father feeds them. And aren't you far more valuable to him than they are? Can all your worries add a single moment to your life? And why worry about your clothing? Look at the lilies of the field and how they grow. They don't work or make their clothing, yet Solomon in all his glory was not dressed as beautifully as they are. And if God cares so wonderfully for wildflowers that are here today and thrown into the fire tomorrow, he will certainly care for you. Why do you have so little faith? So don't worry about these things, saying, "What will we eat? What will we drink? What will we wear?" These things dominate the thoughts of unbelievers, but your heavenly Father already knows all your needs. Seek the Kingdom of God above all else, and live righteously, and he will give you everything you need. So don't worry about tomorrow, for tomorrow will bring its own worries. Today's trouble is enough for today.* (Matthew 6:25–34 NLT)

Everyone goes through trouble, trials, and wilderness seasons, but God fully intended for us to cultivate peace, joy, and contentment regardless of the season we are in. We can always sing our gratitude for His goodness, for God is always good. We can worship Him with songs, hymns, and spontaneous melodies.

> *And everything I've taught you is so that the peace which is in me will be in you and will give you great confidence as you rest in me. For in this unbelieving world you will experience trouble and sorrows, but you must be courageous, for I have conquered the world!* (John 16:33 TPT)

Not only is worrying evidence of unbelief, but it is also a form of worship.

Those Who Believe Enter His Rest

Unfortunately, there is no rest for those who do not believe the Lord and His promises. The unbeliever is vulnerable to unsteadiness and prone to anxiety, as the enemy serves up fear every day.

> *Now the promise of entering into God's rest is still for us today. So we must be extremely careful*

> *to ensure that we all embrace the fullness of that promise and not fail to experience it. ... For those of us who believe, faith activates the promise and we experience the realm of confident rest! For he has said, "I was grieved with them and made a solemn oath, 'They will not enter into my rest.'" God's works have all been completed from the foundation of the world.* (Hebrews 4:1, 3 TPT)

Dr. Brian Simmons, the lead translator of *The Passion Translation*, says in the introduction to the Gospel of John that the word *believe* occurs "nearly one hundred times in John."[9]

> *Beloved friend, I pray that you are prospering in every way and that you continually enjoy good health, just as your soul is prospering.* (3 John 1:2 TPT)
>
> *Don't be pulled in different directions or worried about a thing. Be saturated in prayer throughout each day, offering your faith-filled requests before God with overflowing gratitude. Tell him every detail of your life, then God's wonderful peace that transcends human understanding, will guard your heart and mind through Jesus Christ. Keep your thoughts continually fixed on all that is authentic and real, honorable and admirable, beautiful*

and respectful, pure and holy, merciful and kind. And fasten your thoughts on every glorious work of God, praising him always. Put into practice the example of all that you have heard from me or seen in my life and the God of peace will be with you in all things. (Philippians 4:6–9 TPT)

The Lord gives his people strength. The Lord blesses them with peace. (Psalm 29:11 NLT)

The unbeliever is vulnerable to unsteadiness and prone to anxiety, as the enemy is happy to serve up fear every day.

Joy Thieves

Here's my personal short list of things that steal your joy:

- Anger
- Bitterness
- Fear
- Resentment
- Unforgiveness

- Unrepentance
- Pride
- Jealousy
- Competitiveness
- Strife

Pretty much everything on the entire list is a manifestation of a flesh-driven life versus one being led by the Spirit of God. No one with soundness of mind is intentionally choosing to be hostile toward God. However, a mind that has not been transformed by the Word of God or anyone who is in agreement with the lies of the enemy is hostile toward God. Christians are not exempt from this truth. We all must allow His Word to be our plumb line. "So letting your sinful nature control your mind leads to death. But letting the Spirit control your mind leads to life and peace. For the *sinful nature is always hostile to God.* It never did obey God's laws, and it never will" (Romans 8:6–7 NLT, emphasis added).

> *Put on your new nature, created to be like God—truly righteous and holy. So stop telling lies. Let us tell our neighbors the truth, for we are all parts of the same body. And "don't sin by letting anger control you." Don't let the sun go down while you are still angry.... If you are a thief, quit stealing.*

> *Instead, use your hands for good hard work, and then give generously to others in need. Don't use foul or abusive language. Let everything you say be good and helpful, so that your words will be an encouragement to those who hear them.* (Ephesians 4:24–26, 28–29 NLT)

What will you decide and decree over yourself today? Please allow me to help you with a declaration:

> "Father God, using the authority that You have given me to make great decisions and to pronounce decrees over my life, I decree and declare that the strongholds of fear, anxiety, oppression, and depression are broken off of my life. Lord, please fill me again today with Your precious Holy Spirit, and fill up the spaces where anxiety, fear, oppression, and depression once lodged. Starting right now, I decree that the Lord is my strength and stronghold. Thank You that joy is my portion from You. I will cultivate joy every day, and I will draw from the Holy Spirit's joy, which is residing on the inside of me. I decree and declare that everything that has been lost or stolen is being returned to me even now with restitution in the mighty name of Jesus!"

> *You shall also decide and decree a thing, and it shall be established for you; and the light [of God's favor] shall shine upon your ways.* (Job 22:28 AMPC)

Using Your Free Will Wisely

Our free will was intended to be a blessing; however, whether or not it is, is completely up to us. The Lord invites us to live closely connected to Him by walking in sync with the rhythm of His heartbeat. The wisest choice is to submit our free will to God. "And he gives grace generously. As the Scriptures say, 'God opposes the proud but gives grace to the humble.' So humble yourselves before God. Resist the devil, and he will flee from you" (James 4:6–7 NLT).

All that I have received and experienced from His amazing grace and generosity have been incredibly good. I am all in and honestly desire to know Him more. I want to know His heart and what is on His heart. I want to become His friend by allowing my heart to be moved by what moves His. I want to prove that I love Him by obeying Him more often than not.

The children of Israel were familiar with God's acts but had very little interest in knowing Him or His ways. Assuming they knew Him, they murmured, complained, and accused Him of all sorts of evil. Rebelliously, they even attempted to build new gods using the gold and silver the Lord has just gifted them with. Their foolish stubbornness and rebellion were not only hurtful to God but also kept them from crossing over into the land that God had promised them when He rescued them out of 400 years of slavery. (See Exodus 33:5.)

Knowing the Lord's acts is inferior to knowing Him and His ways. The Lord spoke to Moses "face to face, as one speaks to a friend." Scripture says, "Inside the Tent of Meeting, the Lord would speak to Moses face to face, as one speaks to a friend. Afterward Moses would return to the camp, but the young man who assisted him, Joshua son of Nun, would remain behind in the Tent of Meeting" (Exodus 33:11 NLT).

There are overflowing blessings that come from knowing God, obeying Him, and dwelling with Him in the secret place. Although the Lord's love is unconditional, the blessings listed in Deuteronomy 28 and Psalm 91 are very much conditional.

The blessings of full obedience as listed in Deuteronomy 28 are as follows:

1. The Lord will set us up favorably.
2. Our towns and fields will be blessed.

3. Our children and generations after them will be blessed.
4. Our animals and their offspring will be blessed.
5. We will have plenty of food to eat.
6. Wherever we go, we will be blessed.
7. Whatever we do, we will be blessed.
8. The Lord will conquer our enemies and scatter them in seven directions.
9. The Lord will guarantee a blessing on everything we do and fill our houses with way too many jam-packed blessings.
10. We will be blessed in the land that He is giving us.
11. He will establish us as His holy people.
12. He will give us prosperity in the land that He is giving us.
13. We will have beautiful, flourishing gardens.
14. He will send rain at the proper time.
15. He will bless all of the work that we do.
16. We will lend to many nations, but we will never need to borrow.
17. We will be the head and not the tail.
18. We will be on top and never at the bottom.

Let's take a praise break, lift our hands, and thank God for His loving generosity, which is over the top. Glory to God forever!

According to Kenneth Hagin Ministries, "El Shaddai is one of the seven covenant names through which God revealed Himself to Israel. In Hebrew, it means 'the All-Sufficient One' or 'the God Who is more than enough.'"[10] He is the God of Abraham, Isaac, and Jacob.

If you are a believer, then you have been grafted into God's inheritance by the blood of Jesus. That means that all of the blessings of Abraham, Isaac, and Jacob are yours. (See Romans 11:12–32.)

I understand this sounds *way* too good to be true, so please read it for yourself. Since I am encouraging you to accept and obey the Lord's Way (Jesus) and His grace, mercy, help, and forgiveness, I'm only detailing the good news. I am not listing the curses for rebellion and disobedience. You may read the list of curses for disobedience found in the rest of Deuteronomy 28, if you need extra motivation. The reality is, you are either being transformed by renewing your mind to God's truth and receiving His blessings or you are being enslaved to conform to the rebellious ways of the flesh and inviting curses into your life.

There's nothing unique or liberating about rebellion. Rebellion is as sinful as witchcraft, which is a vicious, dark web that dupes you first before using you to deceive others. Witchcraft, idolatry, and sorcery start as a manifestation in the flesh, which opens the door for the adversary to wreak havoc in your life. "Rebellion is as sinful as witchcraft, and stubbornness as bad as worshiping idols. So because you have rejected the command of the LORD, he has rejected you as king" (1 Samuel 15:23 NLT).

> *When you follow the desires of your sinful nature, the results are very clear: sexual immorality, impurity, lustful pleasures, idolatry, sorcery, hostility, quarreling, jealousy, outbursts of anger, selfish ambition, dissension, division, envy, drunkenness, wild parties, and other sins like these. Let me tell you again, as I have before, that anyone living that sort of life will not inherit the Kingdom of God. But the Holy Spirit produces this kind of fruit in our lives: love, joy, peace, patience, kindness, goodness, faithfulness, gentleness, and self-control. There is no law against these things! Those who belong to Christ Jesus have nailed the passions and desires of their sinful nature to his cross and crucified them there. Since we are living by the Spirit, let us follow the Spirit's leading in every part of our lives. Let us not become conceited, or provoke one another, or be jealous of one another.* (Galatians 5:19–26 NLT)

Bring on the Blessings

If you fully obey the LORD your God and carefully keep all his commands that I am giving you today, the LORD your God will set you high above all the nations of the world. You will experience all these blessings if you obey the LORD your God: Your towns and your fields will be blessed. Your children and your crops will be blessed. The offspring of your herds and flocks will be blessed. Your fruit baskets and breadboards will be blessed. Wherever you go and whatever you do, you will be blessed. The LORD will conquer your enemies when they attack you. They will attack you from one direction, but they will scatter from you in seven! The LORD will guarantee a blessing on everything you do and will fill your storehouses with grain. The LORD your God will bless you in the land he is giving you. If you obey the commands of the LORD your God and walk in his ways, the LORD will establish you as his holy people as he swore he would do. Then all the nations of the world will see that you are a people claimed by the LORD, and they will stand in awe of you. The LORD will give you prosperity in the land he swore to your ancestors to give you, blessing you

> *with many children, numerous livestock, and abundant crops. The* L*ORD will send rain at the proper time from his rich treasury in the heavens and will bless all the work you do. You will lend to many nations, but you will never need to borrow from them. If you listen to these commands of the* L*ORD your God that I am giving you today, and if you carefully obey them, the* L*ORD will make you the head and not the tail, and you will always be on top and never at the bottom. You must not turn away from any of the commands I am giving you today, nor follow after other gods and worship them.* (Deuteronomy 28:1–14 NLT)

Honestly, the best strategy is to rule over your free will from your spirit. In other words, it does not matter what your flesh wants to do or what your mind is telling you to do; it is in your best interest to spiritually run roughshod over your flesh.

The blessings of abiding in the secret place of God, which are listed in Psalm 91, are as follows:

1. The Lord will be your place of safety and trust.
2. The Lord will rescue you from every trap.
3. The Lord will cover and shelter you with the wings of His angels stationed at His throne.

4. You will not be afraid of the terrors of the night or of the arrows (or bullets) that fly in the daytime.
5. Sickness and disaster will not come near you or your home.
6. No evil will touch you or conquer you.
7. No plague will come near your home.
8. The Lord will order His angels to protect you wherever you go.
9. His angels will hold you up and protect your entire body, from head to toe.
10. You will trample and crush your enemies as well as snakes, in the natural realm and in the supernatural realm.
11. The Lord will rescue those who love Him.
12. The Lord will protect those who trust in His name.
13. When you call on the Lord God, He will answer.
14. The Lord will be with you in trouble and rescue you.
15. The Lord will honor you.
16. The Lord will reward you with a long life and give you His salvation.

Practical Life Application

- Stop worrying. Don't lend your imagination to the enemy.
- Don't believe every thought that comes to your mind.
- Visualize yourself in the secret place with God.
- Go from disappointed to reappointed quickly. Practice decreasing the time it takes to spiritually and emotionally self-regulate in an effort to not miss your next appointment with God. Think about God's goodness and lovingkindness and meditate on how He is working behind the scenes.
- Cultivate joy and peace as a lifestyle even during a crisis.
- Consecrate your thought-life to Christ.
- Ask the Holy Spirit for a fresh supply of His Spirit every day.
- Pray in your native language and in the Holy Spirit every day.
- Stay within Jesus's yoke of discipline and remember that He has completed the heaviest part.
- Increase your capacity to receive from your heavenly Father, Jesus, and the Holy Spirit.

- Turn Psalm 51:12 (TPT) into a prayer. Pray that your passion for life will be restored. Pray that you will be able to taste joy in every breakthrough the Lord brings to you. Pray that the Lord holds you close to Him as you willingly obey whatever He says.
- Make declarations like these: "I *will* lend my imagination to the Lord, right in the middle of the drama, problem, or crisis. I will pray, sing, and worship and continue to serve others, especially widows and orphans." "The battle belongs to You, Lord. The believing, trusting, waiting, resting, praying, singing, worshiping, peace, and victory belongs to me!"
- Plead the blood of Jesus over your mind and emotions.

With joy you will drink deeply from the fountain of salvation! In that wonderful day you will sing: "Thank the LORD! Praise his name! Tell the nations what he has done. Let them know how mighty he is! Sing to the LORD, for he has done wonderful things. Make known his praise around the world." (Isaiah 12:3–5 NLT)

- Don't collaborate with the adversary one minute and try to resist him the next minute. He will laugh at you and continue stealing from you. He doesn't stop until you are spiritually, emotionally, or physically dead.
- Use your blood-bought authority.

Counsel in the heart of man is like deep water; but a man of understanding will draw it out. (Proverbs 20:5 KJV)

Chapter 8

A Teachable Heart

A humble heart is a teachable heart. The truth is that every opinion that contradicts the Word of God, including your own, holds no value. It's priceless to understand and believe that you are nothing and can do nothing without God. (See John 15:4–5.)

Pride is the antithesis of humility and hinders our ability to receive wisdom and understanding. Pride also hinders the favor of God from empowering our lives because God opposes or pushes back the proud.

> *And he gives grace generously. As the Scriptures say, "God opposes the proud but gives grace to the humble." So humble yourselves before God. Resist the devil, and he will flee from you. Come close to God, and God will come close to you. Wash your hands, you sinners; purify your hearts, for your loyalty is divided between God and the world. ...*

> *Humble yourselves before the Lord, and he will lift you up in honor.* (James 4:6–8, 10 NLT)
>
> *He said, "You have been given a teachable heart to perceive the secret, hidden mysteries of God's kingdom realm. But to those without a listening heart, my words are merely stories. Even though they have eyes, they are blind to the true meaning of what I say, and even though they listen, they won't receive full revelation."* (Luke 8:10 TPT)

False humility is just as problematic as the classic, in-your-face version of pride, although it prefers to be cloaked. In the end, what will you gain if you manage to sell false humility to a multitude of people? The truth is, the Lord is never fooled. Even the adversary is good at sniffing out false humility. The adversary is eager to help you hide it from others and happy to help you deceive yourself. As I have often heard my favorite mentor and Bible scholar, Dr. Kevin Zadai, say: "satan was the original narcissist!"

As we mature in Christ, we must learn to love what the Lord loves and to hate what the Lord hates. At the top of the list of what the Lord loves is people.

> *"Teacher, which commandment in the law is the greatest?" Jesus answered him, "'Love the Lord your God with every passion of your heart,*

> *with all the energy of your being, and with every thought that is within you.' This is the great and supreme commandment. And the second is like it in importance: 'You must love your friend in the same way you love yourself.' Contained within these commandments to love you will find all the meaning of the Law and the Prophets."* (Matthew 22:36–40 TPT)

The Bible speaks of many things that the Lord loves. Here is a short list of them:

1. The Lord loves all people, which is why He sent Jesus to purchase our salvation with His own blood. (See John 3:16.)
2. The Lord loves people who are "upright in heart and in right standing with Him" (Psalm 146:8 AMPC).
3. The Lord loves a cheerful giver. (See 2 Corinthians 9:7.)
4. The Lord "loves justice" (Psalm 37:28 NLT).
5. The Lord "loves whatever is just and good" (Psalm 33:5 NLT).
6. The Lord loves the people He disciplines. (See Hebrews 12:6.)
7. The Lord "loves the gates of Zion," which is Jerusalem (Psalm 87:2 TPT).

Although the Lord is dedicated and unwavering in His love for us, there remains a list of evil attitudes and behaviors that the Lord hates. It's in our best interest to begin to hate what He hates. Here's a short list:

1. The Lord hates a proud look and putting down others.
2. The Lord hates a lying tongue.
3. The Lord hates hands that shed innocent blood.
4. The Lord hates a heart that manufactures wicked thoughts and plans.
5. The Lord hates feet that are swift in running to evil.
6. The Lord hates a false witness.
7. The Lord hates those who sow discord.

> *There are six evils God truly hates and a seventh that is an abomination to him: Putting others down while considering yourself superior, spreading lies and rumors, spilling the blood of the innocent, plotting evil in your heart toward another, gloating over doing what's plainly wrong, spouting lies in false testimony, and stirring up strife between friends. These are entirely despicable to God!* (Proverbs 6:16–19 TPT)

> *So humble yourselves before God. Resist the devil, and he will flee from you. Come close to God, and God will come close to you.* (James 4:7–8 NLT)

Wisdom Inventory

If you do not respect and honor the one true and living God, Jesus, and the Holy Spirit, go ahead and score yourself with a zero in wisdom, since the very foundation of wisdom is the fear of the Lord. (See Proverbs 9:10.)

> *So don't bother correcting mockers; they will only hate you. But correct the wise, and they will love you. Instruct the wise, and they will be even wiser. Teach the righteous, and they will learn even more.* ***Fear of the LORD is the foundation of wisdom.*** *Knowledge of the Holy One results in good judgment. Wisdom will multiply your days and add years to your life. If you become wise, you will be the one to benefit. If you scorn wisdom, you will be the one to suffer.* (Proverbs 9:8–12 NLT, emphasis added)

Now that the Word of God has cleared up the prerequisite to wisdom, please take an honest inventory of your wisdom. Be sure to also ask the Holy Spirit, who is the Spirit of truth, as the heart is deceitful, for His view.

Ask the Lord, yourself, and a few courageous, kind, mature, stable friends, these questions:

1. Would you describe me as humble?
2. Can you see evidence of Jesus Christ having Lordship over my life and choices?
3. Do you mostly see Jesus or me seated on the throne of my heart?
4. Please provide a few examples that will provide insight.

Every day is an opportunity to make things right with the Lord. We only need to confess to God that we have sinned by missing the mark on His standards, repent for our sins, and ask the Lord to forgive us. No one is exempt from missing the bullseye on God's standards. Prayerfully, as we mature in full surrender and grow in the character of Christ, we are abstaining from practicing blatant sins, so that the enemy won't be successful in deceiving, stealing, and devouring us. "For everyone has sinned; we all fall short of God's glorious standard. Yet God, in his grace, freely makes us right in his sight. He did this through Christ Jesus when he freed us from the penalty for our sins" (Romans 3:23–24 NLT). "But if we confess our sins to him, he is faithful and just to forgive us our sins and to cleanse us from all wickedness" (1 John 1:9 NLT).

Freedom means that we become so completely free of self-indulgence that we become servants of one another, expressing love in all we do. It is love that completes the laws of God.

> *Beloved ones, God has called us to live a life of freedom. But don't view this wonderful freedom as an excuse to set up a base of operations in the natural realm. Constantly love each other and be committed to serve one another. For all of the law can be summarized in one grand statement: "Demonstrate love to your neighbor, even as you care for and love yourself."* (Galatians 5:13–14 TPT)

> *Pride leads to disgrace, but with humility comes wisdom.* (Proverbs 11:2 NLT)

How then does a person gain the essence of wisdom?

> *We cross the threshold of true knowledge when we live in obedient devotion to God. Stubborn know-it-alls will never stop to do this, for they scorn true wisdom and knowledge.* (Proverbs 1:7 TPT)

Freedom means that we become so completely free of self-indulgence that we become servants of one another, expressing love in all we do.

God Is Merciful

Mercy is another manifestation of the Lord's tangible compassion. Not only is He merciful toward us, but He also requires us to extend mercy to others as well. The Lord is never looking for just our intellectual agreement with Him or mere lip service. He is expecting our dedication to Him to be experienced by those around us. It is our responsibility to partner with the Lord and allow Him to heal our brokenness. If you replay painful memories and keep your triggers, you will remain easily hijacked. You will also greatly benefit when you choose to stop clinging to unstable people. Unfortunately, there is no shortage of wounded people through whom the adversary can easily work. You will find them in your family, at your job, at church, and everywhere there are people. Faith requires you to love and forgive every person, yet it is best to build close relationships with the emotionally and spiritually safe, while clinging to Jesus.

...The L*ORD has told you what is good, and this is what he requires of you: to do what is right, to love mercy, and to walk humbly with your God.* (Micah 6:8 NLT)

He is expecting our dedication to Him to be experienced by those around us.

How blessed you are when you demonstrate tender mercy! For tender mercy will be demonstrated to you. (Matthew 5:7 TPT)

Lean on, trust in, and be confident in the L*ORD with all your heart and mind and do not rely on your own insight or understanding. In all your ways know, recognize, and acknowledge Him, and He will direct and make straight and plain your paths.* (Proverbs 3:5–6 AMPC)

Overtaken by Love

It is hard to fathom that the Creator of the universe created us for fellowship with Him. He sees us as His masterpiece, created in His likeness, and He is over-the-top in love!

> *He chose to give birth to us by giving us his true word. And we, out of all creation, became his prized possession.* (James 1:18 NLT)

His perfect, pure love stabilizes us and chases away fear.

> *There is no fear in love [dread does not exist], but full-grown (complete, perfect) love turns fear out of doors and expels every trace of terror! For fear brings with it the thought of punishment, and [so] he who is afraid has not reached the full maturity of love [is not yet grown into love's complete perfection]. We love Him, because He first loved us.* (1 John 4:18–19 AMPC)

The Lord wants us to be filled with His peace, health, and prosperity in every area of our lives. From the Lord's perspective, a loving, connected relationship with us is His top priority. "Beloved friend, I pray that you are prospering in every way and that you continually enjoy good health, just as your soul is prospering" (3 John 1:2 TPT).

The Lord is actually honored when we trust Him. He is stoked to have the short end of the stick in the relationship with us. "Honor me by trusting in me in your day of trouble. Cry aloud to me, and I will be there to rescue you" (Psalm 50:15 TPT).

> *For here is what the Lord has spoken to me: "Because you loved me, delighted in me, and have been loyal to my name, I will greatly protect you. I will answer your cry for help every time you pray, and you will feel my presence in your time of trouble. I will deliver you and bring you honor. I will satisfy you with a full life and with all that I do for you. For you will enjoy the fullness of my salvation!"* (Psalm 91:14–16 TPT)

Practical Life Application

- Believe that God is in love with you and allow His love to heal and transform your life.
- Choose to love yourself and others well.
- Practice humility as a lifestyle.
- Choose the Word of God as your source of truth.
- Believe that you are nothing and can do nothing without God. (See John 15: 4–5.)

❧ Live eager to repent and forgive, and be slow to anger.

Endnotes

Chapter 2

1. *Thayer's Expanded Greek Definition,* s.v. *"alétheia,"* (NT #225), accessed June 10, 2025, https://studylight.org/lexicons/eng/greek/225.html. Emphasis added by the author.

2. *Merriam-Webster.com Dictionary,* s.v. "prudence," accessed June 10, 2025, https://www.merriam-webster.com/dictionary/prudence.

3. *Merriam-Webster.com Dictionary,* s.v. "resiliency," accessed June 10, 2025, https://www.merriam-webster.com/dictionary/resiliency.

Chapter 3

1. Daniel Amen, MD, "Is Your Brain Performing This Critical Process While You're Sleeping?" February 15, 2022, *www.amenclinics.com.*

2. Esin Akay, "The Waste of Creative Talents," L.I.F.E. blog, 16 January 2015, https://esinakay.wordpress.com/tag/george-lands-creativity-test/.

3. Music and lyrics by the author, August 19, 2013.

4. *Strong's Exhaustive Concordance*, s.v. "*ekbasis*," (#G1545), accessed June 12, 2025, https://biblehub.com/greek/1545.htm.

5. *Merriam-Webster.com Dictionary*, s.v. "codependency," accessed June 12, 2025, https://www.merriam-webster.com/dictionary/codependency.

Chapter 4

1. Peter J. Glidden, *The MD Emperor Has No Clothes* (self-published, 2010).

2. Lorna Collier, "Growth after trauma," *Monitor on Psychology*, November 2016, Vol. 47, No. 10, https://www.apa.org/monitor/2016/11/growth-trauma.

3. *Strong's Exhaustive Concordance*, s.v., "*chokmah*," (#H2451), accessed June 12, 2025, https://biblehub.com/hebrew/2451.htm.

4. *Brown-Driver-Briggs Hebrew and English Lexicon*, s.v., "*chokmah*," (#H2451), accessed June 12, 2025, https://biblehub.com/hebrew/2451.htm.

5. *Strong's Exhaustive Concordance*, s.v., "*binah*," (#H998), accessed June 12, 2025, https://biblehub.com/hebrew/998.htm.

6. *Strong's Exhaustive Concordance*, s.v., "*etsah*," (#H6098), accessed June 12, 2025, https://biblehub.com/hebrew/6098.htm.

7. *Strong's Exhaustive Concordance*, s.v., "*geburah*," (#H1369), accessed June 12, 2025, https://biblehub.com/hebrew/1369.htm.

8. *Strong's Exhaustive Concordance*, s.v., "*daath*," (#H1847), accessed June 12, 2025, https://biblehub.com/hebrew/1847.htm.

9. *Strong's Exhaustive Concordance*, s.v., "*yirah*," (#H3374), accessed June 12, 2025, https://biblehub.com/hebrew/3374.htm.

10. *Strong's Exhaustive Concordance*, s.v., "*Yhvh*," (#H3068), accessed June 12, 2025, https://biblehub.com/hebrew/3068.htm.

11. *Strong's Exhaustive Concordance*, s.v., "*kataphroneó*," (#G2706), accessed June 13, 2025, https://biblehub.com/greek/2706.htm.

12. *Merriam-Webster.com Dictionary*, s.v. "HIIT," accessed June 13, 2025, https://www.merriam-webster.com/dictionary/HIIT.

Chapter 5

1. William J. Cromie, "Music on the brain: Researchers explore the biology of music," *Music as Medicine: The impact of healing harmonies*, Material from Longwood Seminars, April 14, 2015, page 41, accessed June 17, 2025, https://hms.harvard.edu/sites/default/files/assets/Sites/Longwood_Seminars/Longwood%20Seminar%20Music%20Reading%20Pack.pdf.

2. "Dr. Sanjay Gupta: Health Benefits of Singing," video clip, Choral Singing in America, accessed June 17, 2025, https://www.youtube.com/watch?v=le2LBDCR43g.

Chapter 6

1. *Vine's Expository Dictionary of New Testament Words*, s.v., "*sarkikos*," (#G4559), accessed June 17, 2025,

https://www.blueletterbible.org/search/Dictionary/viewTopic.cfm?topic=VT0000411.

2. *Strong's Exhaustive Concordance*, s.v., "*sótēria*," (#G4991), accessed June 18, 2025, https://biblehub.com/greek/4991.htm.

Chapter 7

1. *Strong's Exhaustive Concordance*, s.v., "*chay*," (#H2416), accessed June 18, 2025, https://biblehub.com/hebrew/2416.htm.
2. *Strong's Exhaustive Concordance*, s.v., "*panim* or *paneh*," (#H6440), accessed June 18, 2025, https://biblehub.com/hebrew/6440.htm.
3. *Strong's Exhaustive Concordance*, s.v., "*simchah*," (#H8057), accessed June 18, 2025, https://biblehub.com/hebrew/8057.htm.
4. *Strong's Exhaustive Concordance*, s.v., "*yamin*," (#H3225), accessed June 18, 2025, https://biblehub.com/hebrew/3225.htm.
5. *Strong's Exhaustive Concordance*, s.v., "*na'iym*," (#H5273), accessed June 18, 2025, https://biblehub.com/hebrew/5273.htm.

6. *Strong's Exhaustive Concordance*, s.v., "*netsach*," (#H5331), accessed June 18, 2025, https://biblehub.com/hebrew/5331.htm.

7. *Thayer's Greek Lexicon*, s.v., "*sózó*," (NT #4982), accessed June 19, 2025, https://biblehub.com/greek/4982.htm.

8. "The health benefits of strong relationships," Harvard Health Publishing, December 1, 2010, https://www.health.harvard.edu/staying-healthy/the-health-benefits-of-strong-relationships.

9. Brian Simmons, Introduction to John, *The Passion Translation*, 2020 edition (Savage, Minnesota: BroadStreet Publishing Group, 2020), 229.

10. Rhema Team, "El Shaddai," October/November WOF, November 1, 2021, https://events.rhema.org/el-shaddai/.

About the Author

Teri Camp Willis, PhD, ThD, is founder of Love & Willis Family Counseling. She is licensed, commissioned, and board-certified by The National Christian Counselors Association.

Teri is a 1986 graduate of The University of Memphis, having obtained a BBA in Marketing and Advertising. In 2005, she obtained an MA in Clinical Christian Counseling, and in 2007 she graduated with a Doctor of Philosophy in Clinical Christian Psychology, receiving both degrees from Cornerstone University in Lake Charles, Louisiana. In 2024, Dr. Teri completed a Doctorate in Bible and Theology from Warrior Notes School of Ministry.

As a licensed clinical pastoral counselor, Dr. Teri is board certified and provides counseling in the following areas: marriage and family, child and adolescent, and crises and abuse therapies. Teri has written and self-published three books: *Hear the Flowers Sing* is an illustrated children's book, and

Cultivating Joy and *From Diva to Divine* are inspirational mini-books.

Teri is honored to be the mother of one daughter, Taylor Ashley, and her daughter's husband, Jordan.

Dr. Teri is available to bring messages of truth, hope, and encouragement at conferences, workshops, church services, and corporate events. For more information, contact her through:

Drtericampwillis@gmail.com

201-637-8188

www.DrTeriWillis.com

www.ingramcontent.com/pod-product-compliance
Lightning Source LLC
Chambersburg PA
CBHW070036100426
42740CB00013B/2705
9781663102980